THE MONTESSORI FAMILY, THE ULTIMATE STEP-BY-STEP GUIDE FOR AGES 0 TO 5

Create an Empowering Montessori Home Environment and Help Your Child Grow Their Independence, Creativity and Confidence

GRACE STOCKHOLM

TABLE OF CONTENTS

Don't forget to get your complimentary

7 FREE MONTESSORI GAMES FOR THE HOME

(DIY Games for the Kids That Are Worth Your Time!)

(Before you continue to read, make sure to download your complimentary bonus)

In this bonus are a few ideas to help you bring Montessori into your home quickly.

What you'll get:

- 7 free games you can play at home;
- How to use home tools to create the games;
- Specific instructions on how to use the final products with your kids.

The Montessori educational system is ideal for all children!
Follow the link down below to download the games:

http://gracestockholm.net/montessori-education-at-home/

INTRODUCTION

Montessori education has been around for over 100 years and is becoming increasingly popular, especially when well-known public figures like Amazon founder Jeff Bezos, musician Beyoncé Knowles, and Google founder Larry Page lay claim to having received a Montessori education. As a responsible and conscious parent, you want only the best for your child. The traditional, conventional method of education used in schools doesn't always bring out the best in most children. In fact, it can often have a detrimental impact on a child's development. As those children become adults, they are left feeling like they're not enough or that they don't have anything of value to contribute to society. They may not know what they want to do or believe they cannot do it and end up stuck in jobs that aren't suited to them. They may also become driven to succeed due to unmet needs as a child, which ultimately leaves them feeling stressed, burned-out and unfulfilled in their chosen careers.

What Montessori education does is aim to bring out the best in a child from the very start, so they grow up to become balanced, healthy adults. By making the choice to read this book, you are providing yourself and your child with a powerful gift—conscious living. This is what the Montessori method is about, allowing your child to be the conscious, intelligent being they were born to be.

It can be overwhelming and intimidating even to know where to begin with applying Montessori Principles. There is a lot of information out there; trying to take it all in and apply the methods—when you are already a busy parent—may leave you feeling stuck. As a parent who

1

wants only the best for your child and understands the importance of being mindful, you may have found yourself asking the following questions:

- How do I, as a mother, implement Montessori principles at home?
- How can I create a Montessori-like "classroom" for my 0 to 3-year-old?
- What will I need to be successful?
- What are the benefits of Montessori?
- What is my role? What do I need to do? Where do I start?

This book aims to answer those questions. This isn't just a book, it's a guidebook to help you use the Montessori approach in your daily life so you can create a healthy and nurturing environment for your infant or toddler to grow—and be the best they can be in life. One of the amazing things about the Montessori approach is that it doesn't have to be applied only in a school setting; you can use it at home by creating a "classroom" that's suitable for your child to learn in. Does the thought of setting up your home to make it safe, accessible and stimulating for your child seem challenging? Don't worry, it's not! Especially if you use the KISS method: Keep It So Simple. Montessori education centers around creativity, and you can create an environment at home in a way that is cost-effective and stimulating for the child.

In this guide, we will delve deeper into principles you can use and how to implement them. Some things to consider include:

- Respecting the child
- Encouraging children to learn by using their hands
- Slowing down, taking the time to stop and "smell the roses" with your child (literally, too)
- Following the child
- Guiding the child
- Looking at things from their points of view

- Involving the child in daily life
- Refraining from punishing and bribing the child
- Being as prepared as possible by understanding that you will be learning too

With a shift in mindset, you will be pleased to know that successfully implementing Montessori at home is actually straightforward as long as you are well prepared and have a clear understanding of the Montessori approach, your child's development, and enthusiasm to put principles into practice. Just give it a try. There's no need to worry about perfection. It's more important that you are willing to put in the effort and be consistent. If you only attempt to do this method for a day, a week, or a month, then it is not going to stick. It should be done daily to allow the child to adopt new habits and learned behavior.

The great news is that Montessori education does work. The principles have been thoroughly tested by the founder, Dr. Maria Montessori. She was an Italian physician, researcher, and educator who gained a considerable amount of knowledge and understanding of how children interact with their environment and how they learn. She had plenty of opportunities to put her principles into practice, and with each child she guided, she improved and refined her methods. She worked with children from all types of backgrounds, such as those from deprived homes and children with mental, emotional, and/or physical challenges. Time and again her methods proved to be effective. For instance, the Absorbent Mind, a term coined by Dr. Montessori, recognizes that up to the age of six years old, children are very impressionable and absorb everything in their environment. This concept has been researched and proven by scientists. Many researchers throughout the years understand that the first six to seven years of a child's life are crucial, as this period is when their predominant personality traits develop based on programs and conditioning from society. Whatever impressions they receive about themselves and the external environment by the time they are seven, then shapes their personality and the beliefs they hold in the subconscious and unconscious mind. These subconscious patterns are what we operate from well into adulthood, and they determine what we experience. This idea has been known for centuries. Ignatius of Loyola, a man well reputed for his own perspectives on education and human development, states, "Give me the child for the first seven years and I will give you the man."

Scientists from the University of Virginia have found that children who were educated in the Montessori environment outperform children from traditional school settings. Angeline Lillard, from the University of Virginia, who co-led the study, reports,

> Montessori education fosters social and academic skills that are equal or superior to those fostered by a pool of other types of schools... Particularly remarkable are the positive social effects of Montessori education. Typically the home environment overwhelms all other influences in that area. (Lillard, 2006).

The Montessori approach takes into account a child's psychomotor development (changes in the child's motor, cognitive behavior, emotional state and social capacity) from infancy to adolescence. For instance, "floor beds" encourage infants and toddlers to become independent. Dr. Montessori's concept about using floor beds was so effective that today they are widely available for purchase.

The Benefits of Montessori Education

As you read this guide, you will learn about the benefits the Montessori Method provides you and your child. Here are some:

- Your child will learn to become independent very early.
- Your child will be developmentally focused.
- Learning is child-centered.
- This system recognizes that each child is an individual and it is designed to meet their particular needs.
- The method encourages creativity and imagination in the child.
- Montessori fosters social growth, development of emotional

intelligence, and cooperative play.

- Your child will learn self-discipline.
- Your child will learn to focus and concentrate.
- The method encourages self-correction and self-assessment.
- It provides a curriculum that centers around hands-on learning.

There will be many more benefits your child will receive from the Montessori Method that will become noticeable as they grow older. There will be a lasting positive impact on adulthood. Montessori-trained children tend to attract experiences and circumstances that allow for success, independence, and a healthy balance of emotional and mental well-being. They are able to contribute to society, adding value to their communities in a way that they may not have been able to had you chosen to give them a more traditional style of parenting. It makes you wonder, how many people's lives would be happier, healthier, and more productive if they had received education through the Montessori Method?

Studies show that Montessori education in early childhood encourages and grows a child's natural curiosity for their environment. Children tend to be more adept at solving problems and enjoying education, plus they are more prepared socially and academically, according to researchers. The great news is that researchers are able to continue to study Montessori education more thoroughly because many Montessori schools in the USA are now getting public funding, and there is often a waitlist for enrollment! The popularity of Montessori is only gaining.

According to various studies, here are some further outcomes of using the Montessori approach:

- Spiritual awareness—Many Montessori students demonstrate compassion, sensitivity, and empathy to the natural environment.
- They make strong leaders and team members, as they often have a positive impact on their communities.
- Confidence and competence—Montessori students have more confidence, according to research.

- They have original, creative ideas and thoughts.
- They tend to follow internally-grounded thoughts.

Many well-known people who were educated with the Montessori Method believe so strongly in its approach that they support it. For instance, Jeff Bezos has provided $1 billion to fund low-income Montessori preschools. Other well-known Montessorians include:

- Taylor Swift, musician
- Helen Hunt, actress
- His Royal Highness Prince George of Cambridge
- Anthony Doerr, author
- Stephen Curry, basketball player

By reading this book and taking action on the practical recommendations, you will be better prepared to adapt your home environment for the Montessori approach. You will be able to:

- Implement practical tips on using the Montessori way.
- Create a fabulous Montessori home environment.
- Foster early independence for your child from the time they are born to three years old.
- Be an effective guide for your child's healthy development.
- Make sure your child is on track for psychomotor developmental milestones.

Chapter one discusses what the Montessori Method is, including Dr. Maria Montessori's research and the absorbent mind, sensory learning for ages 0 to 3, a child-centered approach (this is what the Montessori Method is based on), guiding principles, your role as a Montessori parent or guardian, and the power of observation. In chapter two, we will then look at the Montessori home by exploring ways you can set up your environment, taking into account the child-centered approach.

This will prepare you for chapter three, where you will discover how to communicate the Montessori way. We will discuss the importance of language and how it relates to Montessori theories of an absorbent mind. We'll delve deeper into language by considering fun activities and emotional learning for the newborn, infant, and toddler. Next, in chapter four, it will be time to take a look at movement and its importance, the brain's connection with movement, and psychomotor development for children 0 to 3 years old. In chapter five, we will look at feeding the Montessori Way by discussing breastfeeding and baby-mother connection, weaning, child-size dishes, and learning table manners.

By the end of chapter six, you will gain a deep understanding of the importance of a safe and clutter-free environment and resisting the urge to plan the child's day. You will learn about Practical Life Activities, a term Dr. Montessori coined. We will also look at ways you can allow the child to explore outside of the home. In chapter seven, we look at socializing and interactions between the child and parent or caregiver. Chapter eight will explore the topic of "sensitive periods" and overcoming the urge or desire to correct the child's behavior. In chapter nine, we will discuss art and music in a Montessori home environment. This is an opportunity to really allow yourself and your child to get creative and have fun! Chapter 10 will help you to make Montessori work for you at home. This chapter will include information about where you can find ideas and inspiration online. Finally, we will wrap up the guide with a conclusion that highlights the important topics discussed.

Congratulations on making this purchase; it is an important and wise decision! In order for children to become successful learners, it is important that they are loved and nurtured so that they can be shaped for success. The Montessori Method's child-centered approach makes for an incredible educational method, and with this guide you will have all the tools to implement it at home straight away. Since the child's brain develops quickly from ages 0 to 3, it's a crucial time for a child's learning, and you have the opportunity to give your child an amazing advantage during this important time.

I urge you not to simply read this book, put it down, and then forget about it. Your child will not benefit that way. Instead, take action and be consistent. The payoff is more than worth it.

CHAPTER 1:

WHAT IS THE MONTESSORI METHOD?

Although the Montessori Method has been around for over 100 years, many people still remain unaware of this pioneering approach to teaching children and believe that the only way children can be (or should be) educated is through the traditional style found in schools. Before we delve deep into the Montessori Method, let's first define what it is.

The Montessori Method was established by Dr. Maria Montessori as an outgrowth of her interest in helping children with special needs or who were at a disadvantage in some way. Unlike in most school classrooms—where teachers prepare and plan the timetable for what the children will learn that day and where they are expected to follow the timetable that has been laid out for them—in a Montessori school, children have the freedom to choose from a variety of activities that they want to focus on. They have the freedom to spend as long as they want on their chosen activity. The teacher or "guide" will simply observe the child's interest and encourage them as much as possible.

Montessori education involves self-direction, hands-on learning, and playing in a way that is collaborative. Children have more creative choices about how they will learn. The teacher, or guide, supports the child's choices by helping to bring out the best in the child with what the child chooses to learn about at any given moment. Children work in groups and individually to learn about the external world and to make further discoveries of their internal world.

Montessori classrooms are deliberately decorated in a way that stimulates and encourages the child's learning through music, science, language, mathematics, social relationships, and much more. Every object and area of a Montessori classroom serves to support and encourage the child's development by focusing on their unique and natural interests.

A Brief History of Dr. Montessori's Research

Dr. Maria Montessori originally had no intention of becoming a teacher and instead set her sights on being a medical doctor. However, the more she worked with children who had intellectual disabilities, the more she realized the children didn't need medical treatment but rather, the ideal type of pedagogy (the method and practice of teaching). She became the director of an orthophrenic school for children with learning difficulties, and soon the children made massive progress in their education. Her curiosity was aroused as she wondered why the educational system seemed to be failing children.

The first Montessori school, opened in 1907, was in Rome. Dr. Montessori was determined to make this "Children's House," as it was called, a place where children from disadvantaged or underprivileged backgrounds could learn, even when many people at the time didn't believe they could. Although at first the children were very challenging to work with, eventually they began to show an interest in some of the activities. For instance, they began to show enthusiasm for puzzles, preparing meals, and tidying their environment, as well as taking part in other hands-on activities. Dr. Montessori noticed that as the children showed an interest in learning these activities, their behavior began to change. They were calmer, more peaceful, were able to concentrate deeply for longer periods, and they showed compassion and kindness towards their environment. The children absorbed information and learned so easily, yet what was really surprising was how they seemed to be teaching themselves!

Dr. Montessori had a strong background in scientific study and also had plenty of experience in working with children from various backgrounds, and this allowed her to design a system for learning that used interesting and unique resources, materials, and ideas that would boost children's desire to learn. Her methods have stood the test of time, as many of them are still used in Montessori classrooms today. When she first opened up the Casa dei Bambini (Children's House), it proved to be so effective that word of mouth spread quickly, and she soon opened up a second school in early 1907 and then the third school later that same year.

After further success across the world, in 1916, Dr. Montessori decided to focus more on educating children who attended elementary school. Many of her training courses and lectures leaned towards educational materials for this age group. She published a book called *L'autoeducazionne nelle Scuole Elementari,* (The Advanced Montessori Method) detailing her opinions and insights into the education of kids between the ages of 7 and 11 years old.

Although her early research focused more on early childhood, by the 1920s she also looked at education for adolescents. What she observed was that at this stage, children required activities and ways of learning that allowed them to explore their true nature, finding themselves and their place in the world. So, she suggested practical activities such as farming, crafting goods with their hands, and then marketing their products. Such activities allowed the children to experience independence and understand the importance of being self-sufficient. These activities also allowed them to gain a deeper understanding of how society is organized and how they could contribute in a positive way.

The Absorbent Mind

When Dr. Montessori introduced the concept of "The Absorbent Mind" to the world, people realized that it plays a crucial role in early childhood development. The absorbent mind is the child's ability to take in what they need from their external environment in order to gain an understanding of their culture and identity. A baby has what is called an unconscious absorbent mind, which means they absorb everything in their environment: the good, the bad and the ugly. It is said that the child's ability to absorb their surroundings so acutely happens up to the age of six or seven. After this time, they begin to develop a logical, reasoning mind, which they carry with them into adulthood. For example, children know how to speak their native language fluently without the need for intellectual and conscious understanding of vocabulary or grammar. Consider this—isn't it interesting how difficult it can be to learn a new language when we are adults or even during our adolescence, and yet it seemed natural and effortless to speak our mother tongue when we were children? Why is this? It's due to the child soaking up the words spoken to them, like a sponge. The child hears the language all the time and begins to associate emotions behind the words, meanings of words, and how they are used in context. This is what the absorbent mind is about, and it allows the child to communicate with others effectively.

As children, we soak everything in, such as our family's traits, habits, belief systems, behavioral patterns, and much more. This is how we learn to develop our character and identity as we grow older. The reasoning mind differs from the absorbent mind because a reasoning mind takes in information consciously and memorizes it. But with the absorbent mind, we take things in unconsciously, and it involves very little effort on our parts. Neuroscientists often refer to the absorbent mind as the subconscious/unconscious or the Theta brainwave state, which is what we primarily operate in up to the age of six or seven years old. As we grow older, we are mainly operating in the Beta brainwave state (the conscious or reasoning mind). However, what young children have learned through their absorbent minds still shapes their characters and personalities.

Dr. Montessori understood the power of the absorbent mind, and you can be amazed by it, as well. It allows you as a Montessori parent or guardian to prepare a deeply nourishing and empowering environment for your infant or toddler.

Sensory Learning 0 to 3

Dr. Montessori believed that our knowledge and intellect play an important part in opening up our sensory perception. After all, we use our senses of sight, smell, touch, sound, and taste to gain a better understanding of our surroundings and ourselves. We use these five senses to collect data and stimulate us to deepen our knowledge.

> The senses, being explorers of the world, open the way to knowledge. Our apparatus for educating the senses offers the child a key to guide their explorations of the world. They cast a light upon it, which makes more things visible to them in greater detail than they could see in the dark, or uneducated state. (Montessori, 1949).

You will see how Dr. Montessori's ideas on how the senses affect the development of the intellect can be put into practice later in this guide.

The key for guides in a Montessori program is providing materials that activate the child's senses in deeply stimulating ways.

Dr. Montessori's ideas about developing sensory learning in young children were inspired by the works of French educator Edouard Seguin, who worked with intellectually and mentally challenged children. Since Dr. Montessori first started out working with children who were not receiving sufficient sensory stimulation, she had the opportunity to observe and experiment with ways to positively influence their sensory development. Even to this day, research is still being carried out in this field, and there is much more to learn. Still, Montessori's research was ground-breaking, and she created materials called Sensory Education. This form of education was developed to allow kids to learn through their senses and enhance their intellectual development. There is a particular period for children between the ages of 0 to 3 years old when their sensory input is extra sensitive. This is a time when the child is interested in developing their learning and understanding with a particular skill or knowledge.

To give you a deeper understanding of sensitive periods, here are some of the most recognized ones:

- Movement (0 to 6 years)
- Language (0 to 5)
- Order (1 to 3.5)
- Music (2 to 6)
- Toilet training (1 to 1.5)
- Socializing (2.5 to 5)
- Sensory Skills (0 to 6)

We will dive deeper into sensitive periods in chapter eight.

A Child-Centered Approach

Dr. Montessori strongly believed that a child should be able to take their own learning needs and focus on them rather than being told or dictated to by a teacher about what they should be learning. Her bias in this respect has been validated over time as the results are evident even to this day that her ideas and concepts do work. She understood that extra care and attention must be given to children in their early years (from birth to 6 years old) if they are to become capable, healthy, balanced adults who know their own worth and have a strong sense of self. With this approach, children are encouraged and supported in developing in the areas of their learning needs. They take charge of what they want to explore, and teachers/guides observe the cues and encourage children accordingly. This approach is also known as "play-based" and gives the infant or toddler space to learn at their own pace rather than feeling forced to go at the same pace as everyone else, which is what tends to happen in a traditional educational style of teaching.

A child-centered approach allows infants and toddlers to have fun while learning, and it enables learning in an unstructured way. We will discuss this further in the guide. In order to adopt a child-centered approach, it's important to:

1. Develop a curriculum that focuses on the unique needs, natural gifts, interests and strengths of the child.
2. Ensure that the child's environment and experiences reflect their particular learning needs.
3. Have the infant or toddler develop fine motor skills, language skills, and motor coordination.
4. Develop confidence in the child's abilities as they begin to emerge.
5. Find ways to encourage the child to make decisions and confidently choose to focus on their desired activities.
6. Allow the infant or toddler to self-direct their play, as this teaches them to become independent and trust their choices.
7. Create opportunities for the child to further explore their creativity and develop problem-solving skills.

Guiding Principles

Here are key principles that are important for you to understand as a Montessori parent or guardian.

A Child Is Free To Explore the Environment

When the environment has been well-prepared, it allows for optimal growth and learning for the child. This environment includes the child, you, and the physical components, such as Montessori equipment, materials, and apparatus. There are six aspects of this environment, which are: **beauty, structure and order, freedom, social interactions, nature and reality**, and **intellectual stimulation**.

- Montessori environments need to be beautiful but simple. This means no clutter. The environment should be peaceful, safe, clean, and well-kept.

- Structure and order allow the child to better understand their surroundings and come to the realization that there is also structure and order in the universe. So, it's not about creating a strict regime or schedule, but rather, it's about microcosm and macrocosm. As mentioned earlier, the sensitive periods are an excellent opportunity for the child to understand structure and order because during this time (ages 0 to 3), they start to draw conclusions about their surroundings.

- In the Montessori approach, we allow the child to have freedom of movement, choice, social interaction, and exploration.

- With a healthy social environment, the child can interact with other people (both adults and children) freely. As they get older, they will be socially confident rather than suffering from social anxiety, which is more likely to happen in a non-Montessori environment.

- Nature and reality are important, and it is said that Dr. Montessori loved being in nature and had the greatest respect for it. She strongly advised taking children out into nature and not just have them stay inside all the time. Even today, many educators, guides, mentors, coaches, and parents understand the importance of children being in nature. Both adults and children benefit enormously when they have gotten into the habit of surrounding themselves by nature. When your infant or toddler is exposed to nature and reality often, this will significantly boost their health, mentally, emotionally, and physically. This is why natural materials, instead of synthetics, are ideal for a Montessori environment. For example, expose the child to real wood, glass, bamboo, reeds, cotton, and metal.

- If the above aspects are integrated into the environment, then it will allow for a stimulating intellectual environment.

A Child Is Master of His/Her Own Learning

Dr. Montessori first discovered the possibility that children have the ability to learn naturally when she walked past a desolate child who was absorbed in playing with a red piece of paper. It got her thinking, though what exactly was going through her mind, we'll never know for certain. Perhaps it was the child's ability to focus so intently, or maybe she thought the child had an ability to learn. Either way, this simple incident was enough to encourage her to carry on with her studies. She discovered that children naturally and effortlessly reach out for knowledge. They explore and create, but what she found most interesting was just how much focus and attention a child can put into learning. As she watched children, she noticed that they thrived on learning new things and would become completely engaged in their tasks. There was a child who was so engrossed in what she was doing that even when Montessori got the other children to play music and dance around the girl, she wasn't distracted. Montessori even proceeded to lift the child up, and still, she remained engrossed in what she was doing. If we let children take control of their learning, they instinctively know what is right for them to learn, and they become masters at it!

A Child Learns Through His/Her Senses

Using the five senses we have mentioned, children can educate themselves with their environment. This is why it's essential that the ideal environment is set up.

A child Needs a Safe and Nurturing Environment

A child has the desire to adapt to the environment because doing so allows him to gain a better understanding of himself and also gives meaning to the world around him.

The Role of the Montessori Parent

It is necessary that you are clear on what role you are to play as a Montessori parent. It is the role of a guide. It requires the right kind of balance, though. For instance, it's not about being their boss with a "do as I say or else" attitude. And on the other hand, you're not a servant, so it's important not to take the "I'll do everything for you" approach. Both of these mindsets work against the Montessori approach.

The Parent As Guide

The roles carried out by the parent, teacher, and child are equally important, essential, and unique. As an observer, caregiver, and guide, you, the parent, are offering your child a private and intimate education in a way that cannot be done outside of the home. According to *A New Generation of Evidence: The Family is Critical to Student Achievement* (a report by the National Committee for Citizens in Education),

> The evidence is now beyond dispute. When schools work together with families to support learning, children tend to succeed not just in school, but throughout life. In fact, the most accurate predictor of a student's achievement in school is not income or social status, but the extent to which that student's family is able to:
>
> 1. Create a home environment that encourages learning
> 2. Express high (but not unrealistic) expectations for their children's achievement and future careers
> 3. Become involved in their children's education at school and in the community. (Berla and Henderson, 1994)

It is not just the child who will be learning through studying, but you too. It's your role as a guide to study and gain a deep understanding of the Montessori principles and how your child is developing. You will learn by observation. Ask yourself how your child is responding to what is in their environment and how can you continue to encourage and support them. First, though, you must create the right environment that is safe and allows opportunities for your child to explore.

Attunement and Attention

It's vital that as their guide, you are able to pay attention to how your child is responding to their chosen activities. Attunement and attention are fantastic skills to develop and something you'll be able to do as you practice the Montessori methods. The more tuned in you are to your child's needs, the easier it will be for you as a guide because you'll know how to respond to their learning requirements. Something to bear in mind is that when children know you're tuned in and paying attention while they explore their environment, it helps to boost their confidence and encourages their desire to learn more. It can be disheartening for children if they realize that their parents or guardians are too busy or too distracted to pay attention to the activities that interest them. So, allowing yourself to become attuned and attentive will enhance the bond between you and your child.

The Power of Observation

In a Montessori classroom, teachers spend a lot of time observing the child in order to support them with their learning. Likewise, it's important that you do this in the home. This involves watching the child to see how they interact with various materials and people. When teachers do this in the classroom, it helps them to gain a better understanding of the child's character and how they learn. Observing your child in this way will benefit you enormously as the child's guide. Observation will be a valuable tool for you. As an example, you could watch how your child plays independently. What causes boredom easily? What causes frustration? What brings excitement, amusement or happiness? Trying to find the answers to these questions will enable you to create activities that cater to the child's preferences.

You might think of an observer like being a scientist or researcher who is carrying out scientific study and data collection. This is an opportunity to have fun and become really curious. Keep a notepad or audio recorder with you to make notes on your observations. Ideally, you will need to take an objective approach. Pretend you don't know your child and make notes from this point of awareness. Try and set aside your judgments, opinions, preconceived notions, and expectations, and just allow yourself to be present with what is going on with your child. Make your notes in objective language. For example, "Katie read the book twice," rather than, "Katie really likes the book."

So you don't feel overwhelmed, you can choose to focus on one thing at a time and write down everything in that area. Here are some things you can observe:

- Fine and gross motor movement
- Eating
- Emotions
- Communication
- Sleeping
- Socializing

Once you have plenty of information on your observations, it will be easier for you to decide what you might want to do next. For instance, you may decide to provide your child with more challenging puzzles, teach them to go up or down the stairs, or slow down with a particular activity so that they can better learn it. Or you may decide that a particular area doesn't require any further action at that time.

CHAPTER 2:

THE MONTESSORI
HOME ENVIRONMENT

The environment you create for your child should be safe, simple, clean, and should contain beauty. In this chapter, we will delve deeper into how you can start to create this ideal environment.

Setting Up the Montessori Environment

You may want to jot down ideas on how you can start to set up the environment. You may not know what materials you want to use, which is why it helps to keep things simple. Carefully select a few activities to start with; you can always offer a few more later once you have carried out your "scientific research." To help keep things organized, you could store and rotate activities and toys. You could store away most of the activities but leave out on display a few of your child's favorite ones to start with and only bring in the others once the child has become bored with the existing ones. Remember to place any unused activities in a box so that the environment remains uncluttered and safe.

The Importance of a Child-Centered Environment

As you begin to think about the environment for your child, remember to keep in mind that it's a good idea to select tasks that are:

- Related to their interests,
- Quite challenging,
- Meaningful to them.

This will help to create curiosity in the child. It's important that you take into account what they might be interested in learning rather than what you think they should be learning. Your preferences for your child may differ from theirs, and if you try to force your desires onto them, that strategy will likely backfire!

Part of what makes a child-centered environment is having uninterrupted work periods. It will allow the child to work in their own space and at their own pace, which will provide the time to complete the task, tidy up, and then start the next activity. Order is essential because "..the small baby cannot live in disorder. Disorder disturbs him, upsets him, and he may express his suffering by despairing cries, or by an agitation that can even assume the forms of illness" (Montessori, 1936).

Child-size items

It's important to set up your home to make it as accessible as possible for your child. Now is the time to grab your notepad and start jotting down a list of appropriate furniture and materials you may want to consider. There's a further resources section at the back of this book that contains information on where you can purchase goods.

Child-appropriate sizes will encourage independence, creativity, enthusiasm, and problem-solving. Take a good look around for small cleaning tools such as mops, watering cans, a dustpan, and broom. Drawers are a good option so the child can store things away. You may also want to consider cups such as plastic or stainless steel for infants and toddlers. However, the reason glass cups are encouraged is because if the child drops plastic cups, they are more inclined to believe they can drop things and nothing will happen. If they drop a glass, however, well, that's a more serious consequence.

Ability to reach items

It's essential that the child has items placed at their level so they can reach them easily and effortlessly. Here are some examples of things you can make accessible to the child: low hooks for their coat and bag, cleaning materials, baskets for arranging things, plant and flower pots for when they need to water them, and trays. Ensure that wherever their activities are stored, they're accessible to the child. Otherwise, they will need to depend on you every time they want to take something out or put it away.

Mirror

A mirror should also be accessible and placed so that it's at the child's level. Babies and toddlers are intrigued by mirrors, and when they get the opportunity to look into one, it helps them to discover their identity and observe their movements. We recommend purchasing a mirror that isn't breakable, with a wooden frame which will allow the child to hold on for balance and walk along it.

The Floor Bed

In a traditional-style nursery setting there will be a crib. However, in a Montessori environment we use a floor bed. This allows the child to experience full freedom to move around the room (providing it is childproof). A crib restricts the child's independence and therefore isn't in alignment with the Montessori environment. A floor bed, on the other hand, gives the child the option to be on it or not.

Some Montessori parents prefer to keep their babies in a Moses basket or something similar during the newborn stage, and then they move on to using a floor bed. There is often debate and controversy as to whether or not a child should be put in a floor bed. This is due to many people being conditioned to believe that a crib is the safest option until the child is ready for a bed. You may be asking, what if my child constantly gets out of the floor bed? Will it not be dangerous? It is important that you ensure wherever the floor bed is kept, the room *must* be childproof first.

In order to do this, perhaps it would be a good idea to get onto your child's level, literally. Get down on your hands and knees and check for anything or anywhere that may prove to be a hazard.

Once you're confident the room is completely safe, then you can put the floor bed in there. As for whether your child will be able to sleep on the floor bed, it depends on the child. Some Montessori parents find they work just fine and the toddlers or infants sleep soundly. Other parents find that their child keeps getting in and out of bed. It depends on your child's sleep patterns and their sleep history. If they are prone to restless sleep patterns, are highly energetic and persistent, then there's a chance they may be hopping in and out. On the other hand, if your child is trained to use a floor bed very early on, then they may find it comfortable and not think anything of it. I encourage you to explore this further. You won't know until you try.

If you find your child sleeps just fine with the floor bed, then we encourage you to stick with it. If it doesn't appear to be working for your child, then you can either be patient until they get used to it and settle into a sleep pattern, or it may be the case that they are better off transitioning to a crib.

If you're looking for a more cost-effective solution to a floor bed, you can simply place a mattress on the floor. It works just as well!

Furniture

Child-size table and chairs

The furniture that you'll generally find in stores is too big for infants and toddlers. It's important to look for chairs and tables that allow your child's feet to reach the ground comfortably. If they're uncomfortable, they won't feel at peace. You may need to cut down the table and chair legs, depending on the size of your child. A significant benefit of having the furniture be child-size is that it means the child isn't reliant on the adult to be able to carry out activities or move around.

Wooden stepstool

This is ideal for the child to be able to step up and use the sink or reach something else that may be a little too high for them. Ideally, find one that's easy to clean, meets strict standards for design, and will be comfortable for the child to use.

Glider/Rocker for Breastfeeding

Here's the difference between the two: A glider is similar to an armchair that makes you and your child feel like you could be floating. Many parents find a glider to be comfortable as it comes with cushions. You also have the option to keep your feet up with a stool in front of it. A rocker enables you to rock your baby up and down. It's also known to be comfortable and babies tend to find the rocking sensation a terrific sleeping aid. So, as to which one you should use, it's entirely up to you.

A Child's Corner in Different Rooms of the House

While you may decide to dedicate a room to being a Montessori environment, if you can have at least a corner in other areas of the house to serve as your child's corner, all the better. Even just a small change in a room can make a huge difference to your child's behavior. This is your opportunity to get creative with how you want to dedicate a corner in different parts of the house. Creating a Montessori environment in your home can be a lot more challenging than creating it in a school classroom, but it can certainly be done. As mentioned previously, it's essential to keep it simple. This will also help you so that you're not overwhelmed with all the changes you feel you need to make. It may involve you giving your home a detox so that it is uncluttered. Before you make a start in designing a Montessori environment, just go through the house (one room at a time) and give it a good declutter. Once you have done this, it will be much easier for you to implement the Montessori approach. It's like starting with a blank slate.

Depending on the layout and space of your home, you may decide to have just a small section or corner dedicated to your child. This is a great way for the child to learn that they have their own space/s in the home. For instance, one corner of the house could be turned into the "quiet" space corner or "peace" corner, where they can go to be reflective. You could decorate the corner with a plant or flower pot, a fish tank, or a calming piece of artwork, etc. If you have a toddler or infant, it would be a great idea to let them contribute to the decoration or creation of their corner/s. You may decide that the "peace" corner is a window where the child can simply sit quietly and look outside. Remember to childproof/babyproof every room in the house.

Montessori Materials

It can be very easy to get caught up in the materials you want to buy or feel you need to purchase. You can go on a mad shopping spree and find you've bought too much. Again, I would like to remind you to keep it simple, not only for your sake but for the child's. That said, it's advisable that you purchase or create certain things such as child-size items and furniture that is safe for the child. Additionally, here are some materials you might want to consider:

Mobiles

These are a fantastic way to encourage newborn babies. They not only help with development but also excitement. A mobile is a toy that is placed above the baby's head and acts as a visual stimulation to encourage brain development. There are different types of mobiles; some are intended for stimulation and others are meant to be used as a sleeping aid.

- If your baby is approximately three to six weeks old, a **Munari** mobile might be a good way to go. This is a black and white mobile that is made with geometrical shapes because the baby isn't able to see color yet. It also has the benefit of exposing the newborn to linear and curvilinear shapes. Since it moves slowly, it gives the child the opportunity to focus on observing it in action.

- If your baby is approximately six to eight weeks old, an **Octahedron** mobile is suitable. It allows the baby to understand geometric proportions, patterns, and relationships. It consists of three colors—red, blue, and yellow—to give the baby an idea of basic colors.

- At seven to ten weeks old, the baby is ready for a **Gobbi** mobile. It is light enough to be moved by the air and is made of five balls, colored the same but in different shades. This design allows the child to understand the different shades of a color and also the depth of field as the balls are raised higher and higher. The balls move gently and will likely keep the baby fascinated for quite some time.

Some parents like to make their own mobiles, or you can purchase them ready-made online (see further resources section at the back of the guide).

Rattles

When your infant is around three months old, you may want to let your child experience a rattle. Rattles give your baby the chance to move, and this helps to develop their motor skills, strengthens their muscles, gives practice with their grip, and it can even be used as a teething toy. You can always start the baby off with a simple wooden rattle and then move on to colorful rattles (though there is nothing wrong with this from the start). The important thing to remember is to only change when the baby loses interest in the existing one. You may decide to use household objects as "rattles," like wooden spoons, etc. If you like to get creative, perhaps you can come up with ways you can transform safe household items into suitable rattles.

Puzzles

Puzzles work well for babies and older children. Susan Mayclin

Stephenson, author of The Joyful Child: Montessori, Global Wisdom from Birth to Three, suggests:

> "This is the time to give very simple shape and colour puzzles as children love to put things inside containers, such as puzzle pieces in spaces that match."

(Stephenson, (2013).

There are a variety of puzzles for each age group. The following is an example that other Montessori parents have found helpful to introduce their child to puzzles:

- At around eight months old, you could start the child's first puzzle with an **egg and cup** because at this stage your child is likely able to sit up and move their arms.

- Once they have mastered the egg and cup, you could try **palmer and pincer grasp blocks**. This type of puzzle allows the child to develop their motor skills with coordination of the index finger and thumb. This is a milestone for the baby and helps to lay the foundation for the fine motor movements of the fingers and hand. For instance, whenever you pick up a pen you are using the pincer grasp.

- At around nine months old, the child can be introduced to **single shaped puzzles** that consist of the circle, square, and triangle. Why not start them with the circle first, as that is the easiest of the shapes to master because it can move in any direction. Next, have them try the square and then a little later (between 10 to 11 months), they are likely ready to use the triangle. One of the benefits of these puzzles is that they allow the child to develop their hand-eye coordination skills.

- Around 11 months old, they may be ready to work with **three shape puzzles** where the pieces are different sizes. For example, you could try them with the Montessori Three Circles Puzzle or Rectangle Sorter, which can be purchased online (see further resources section).

- Once your child is around 12 to 14 months old, you can

consider introducing more complex shape puzzles. Some of these have five shapes, and others have similar shapes but in different sizes.

- Finally, at around 14 to 18 months old, your child can be introduced to **chunky puzzles**. Some examples are puzzles that feature the shapes of animals, fruits, or vehicles. You may find that your child will benefit from chunky puzzles that have knobs. They have lifelike images that will keep the child entertained as well as allowing them to learn. Also, because the puzzles have knobs, they help to support the pincer grasp.

Wooden Toys/Natural Materials

The Montessori approach encourages the use of wooden and natural materials. Inside a Montessori classroom, there are very few things that are made from synthetic materials. Dr. Montessori was a strong advocate for nature and all things natural. She believed that children should be inspired by and can learn a lot from nature, which is why she recommended that the classroom and most materials for children be made from natural materials such as bamboo, real wood, metal, cotton, and glass. Most Montessori stores offer toys and equipment that are made from wood.

As stated at the beginning of the guide, it's a good idea to keep things simple. Although many Montessori toys are made from wood, they are simple and not flashy. Nevertheless, they are powerful tools to help your child learn and have fun at the same time.

Floor Mats

Dr. Montessori didn't think it is a healthy approach for children to sit down and learn at hard desks and chairs for several hours a day, every day. She then chose to bring in small tables and chairs because they are light enough for a child to move around with. Work mats were introduced into the Montessori Method because children like to play on the floor, spread out, roll about, and lie on their tummies while being absorbed in their learning. The floor mat also serves as an opportunity for young children to get a good sense of external order in their immediate environment. For instance, the child is less likely to throw their work all over the place if they are working calmly on the floor. It teaches the child intention and discipline.

You can use a floor mat to help your infant to develop spatial awareness. It will also help with body strength and balance. A floor mat is also a great way to help the child roll the mat so it can be put away. In addition, the floor mat will help the infant or toddler to develop their own space and is very useful to have if you decide to place your infant in front of the mirror. The mat is a safe space for the child to look at himself in the mirror.

Buying Ready-Made Materials Versus Homemade Materials

When it comes to having Montessori materials, you can either purchase them or do it yourself, if you feel drawn to do so.

There is no right or wrong way with how you decide to set up your Montessori home. If you are on a budget and you happen to be creative, then you can put that creativity to use with how you design the Montessori environment. Actually, being creative is a great way to set the foundations since the Montessori approach is all about encouraging creativity.

High cost of ready-made materials

One of the problems many Montessori parents face is the high costs of purchasing ready-made materials. One of the reasons the costs are high for Montessori products is because they are of a higher quality. The items are made from real wood and other natural materials which are not really mass-produced. Many of these toys come with a high level of craftsmanship, too. You may find that once you start to make a list of the furniture and other items you'd like to have in your home environment, costs begin to mount. However, bear in mind that less is more with the Montessori Method and you don't need a box full of toys. A handful of high-quality toys for your child will be more beneficial than lots of lower-quality ones.

You may also be wondering how you can create a Montessori environment without jeopardizing the approach. Please do not allow the expense to cause you any stress, as there are many parents who have found a way around this. Just remember, this is a fantastic opportunity to think outside of the (toy) box and get creative. Even if you don't consider yourself to be creative, you may be surprised at what you come up with as wonderful alternatives to store-bought items. As is often the case in this realm of creativity and do-it-yourself, Pinterest is an infinite resource for inventive, simple, and actionable ideas.

Homemade alternatives (make-your-own)

There are plenty of online communities where parents share tips and advice on how they create and maintain a Montessori Method on a budget (see further resources). Here are some tips for creating an environment on a budget. What ideas can you also come up with?

- Modify existing materials you have. Even if your budget doesn't currently allow you to have certain materials or equipment, you can still modify what you have. For instance, you could use wooden utensils as toys for your baby or infant.

- Use nature. If you aren't able to bring nature into your home in a big way, why not go outside? Explore the outdoors with your child, which is free and deeply enriching for both of you. You can find creative games to play with your child while you're in nature; this applies to babies as well as toddlers and infants. Why not have your child make footprints in the mud, create a treasure hunt, or find different types of seeds, plants or animals?

- Why not join a Montessori for Parents Community and suggest swapping toys or materials?

- Make a wish list of the things you would like. You never know who may gift you with them!

Here are some suggestions on how you can make your own:

- Can you find ingredients in your kitchen that could be used for scientific experiments and cooking classes?
- Rather than purchase flashcards, why not make your own Montessori inspired cards on topics such as Mathematics, Science, English, and History?
- You can also go out into nature and see what natural materials you can find that will serve well to help you make your own or that you could just take home.
- Use recycled materials.

DIY fine motor skills activities

Please keep in mind that as a parent, you are the best judge as to whether your child is ready for certain toys and activities based on your observations in daily life. The below is a guide that aims to inspire you on what you can create, but always tune in to see if it feels right for your child.

1. You just need a parmesan shaker and some drinking straws or match sticks. Give them to your child so that they can be occupied in playing with the materials. Alternatively, using a bowl with holes, so that your child could insert the match sticks or drinking straws into the holes to make a hedgehog!
2. Playdough or plasticine is very cheap and excellent for developing fine motor skills for infants and toddlers. For instance, children can cut, roll, mold, pinch, poke, and find other ways to shape the playdough or plasticine. They can use their imaginations with what they want to create. Once they have created something, they can start again and make something else. There are many websites and YouTube videos that offer inspiration on what can be created with playdough or plasticine.
3. Perhaps your child might enjoy threading household items, including dry pasta, plasticine, twigs, beads, and rings.

4. You can use materials such as beads, pasta, stones, or whatever materials you choose. Get a small bowl and a divided tray or plate. Put one of each item into each part or section of the divided tray/plate and transfer the rest of the items into the bowl, making sure they are mixed up well. Then ask your infant or toddler to sort out the items in the bowl by matching them up to the corresponding item in the divided tray.

5. Color gradient toys. You could get an empty egg carton and color each egg slot differently. Then find items with corresponding colors (such as Lego blocks or use corks and just paint them) and ask your infant to match up the items to the correctly colored egg slot.

If you'd prefer to purchase items ready-made, that's absolutely fine too. Just remember not to purchase so much that you end up with a cluttered environment. We always want to apply the KISS (Keep It So Simple) method.

CHAPTER 3:

COMMUNICATING THE MONTESSORI WAY

When we talk to babies (and pets), we naturally communicate with them in a high-pitched, animated way. It's intuitive; we just seem to be aware that this is an appropriate way to connect with them. It's important to remember that babies and infants hear differently than adults do. According to researchers at the University of Washington, babies hear all frequencies simultaneously. It's a good idea to talk to your baby or toddler in a high-pitched voice because they hear high-pitched tones in humans better. It is difficult for babies to hear tones because their hearing hasn't fully developed yet. What this means is that the ways that we communicate with children can differ according to the environment. Lynne Werner, a Professor of Speech and Hearing Sciences at the University of Washington notes that

> If you are a baby, it is sensible to listen broadband, and it was valuable for our ancient ancestors for survival in the Serengeti (the Serengeti Plain of Eastern Africa). But in today's western culture a baby is at a great disadvantage. All the noise we expose people to makes it difficult for babies. The practical lesson from this research is, if you are talking to a baby or reading them a story, background noise can be a problem. Turn off the television or radio. (2001)

Once the baby becomes a child, they have grown out of the "motherese" language phrase and need to be spoken to like any person. Remember, babies absorb everything that's taking place in their surroundings. If they are constantly being exposed to people talking "normally" rather than in "motherese," they will pick this up and it will allow them to start speaking their native language fluently too. It's okay to use big words around your baby because, although they won't understand what the words mean at this stage, they will naturally start to use those words as part of their vocabulary when they can speak more fluently. They may ask you what the word/s mean, and you can explain or encourage them to use a dictionary by sitting down together and looking up the definition.

Language and an Absorbent Mind

Communicating with your child involves more than just using certain words and tone of voice. It's also about your demeanor, attitude, body language, and your reactions to why the child is responding to you. For example, if your child is under three years old, how you respond to them in daily life greatly affects their confidence and trust. If you respond positively and acknowledge their needs, you will enhance their trust in you as a parent and build their confidence in social interactions. They will feel it's safe to move around and explore their environment.

Since the very early years of a child's life is a sensitive period, when you use rich language in the home, they soak this up like a sponge. You are laying the foundations for later years. A home that is rich in language will help to give the child a rich vocabulary further down the line. Dr. Montessori stated,

> Not only does he create his language, but he shapes the organs that enable him to frame the words. He has to make the physical basis of every moment, all the elements of our intellect, everything the human being is blessed with. (1949, p. 22)

During this stage of a child's life, the Montessori approach advocates introducing the child to a rich language that consists of music, science, math, art, and geometry.

Naming Items

Since we know that toddlers are in their sensitive period, it's a perfect opportunity to make good use of developing their language skills. Do remember that they are much smarter than we may give them credit for, and they will soak in everything they hear, see, touch, taste, and feel.

Talk to them in complete sentences. When you encourage them to start naming items, point to the item and speak clearly. Try not to use slang, and don't be afraid of using big words! It's a good idea at this stage to be quite descriptive or at least elaborate a bit more than you would have when the child was a baby. For example, rather than pointing to a ball and saying "ball," why not say something like, "it's a big, round, blue ball." The human interaction will help to give the item more meaning to the child but also encourages their interaction.

The more specific you can be when naming items, the better. Rather than saying, "it's a red car," why not say instead, "it's a red Ferrari." This arouses their curiosity and encourages them to ask more questions. Try using medical and scientific terms too. For instance, rather than saying, "it's a flower," you could instead say, " it's a tulip."

Narrative Activities

Using narrative to help develop your child's language skills may seem obvious even outside of the Montessori environment, and one cannot underestimate just how relevant storytelling is. Applying narration can be used to introduce the child to new concepts as well as reinforce existing ones. Even in adults, scientists are aware of the changes in the brain when we listen to stories instead of hearing a lecture that's full of facts and figures. Could it be because stories tend to engage us emotionally? We can identify and relate to characters in a story, which allows us to build a stronger connection with the storyteller. Narrative activities will help to deepen your child's capacity for compassion and empathy, as well as increase their focus and attention span.

Here are suggestions on how to make the most of narrative activities:

1. **Hand rhyme.** When you are telling a story or nursery rhyme, it's a good idea to demonstrate the story with your hands and encourage your child to do the same. This will encourage interaction and will engage their senses.

2. **Watch nature and tell a story around it.** Even if it's raining outside (especially if it is), see if you can find somewhere that is sheltered. You can just sit or stand by the window inside your home, or simply go outside wearing waterproofs and talk to the child about what's happening around you. For instance, talk about what's happening with the flowers, bugs, trees, grass, and anything else you can see. This helps them to tune into different points of view. It will stimulate their imagination. If you prefer, just listen to the rain and various sounds.

Reading Books

Books that are suitable for your child at this stage (babies, toddlers and infants) include:

- Picture books
- Alphabet books
- Books with real-life pictures
- Audiobooks
- Sensory books
- Books that introduce numbers

Since the child is still trying to make sense of their environment and themselves, Dr. Montessori advised that for children in their early years, it's a good idea to look for books that focus on reality. Here's an idea of the type of books that are suitable for each age range (this may differ depending on the unique learning needs of your child):

1. **Birth to 18 months - Black and White books:** These types of books have black and white images. You can purchase ones where the images fold out (pop-ups) and stand up so your child can look at them without your assistance.

2. **Art for baby books:** These types of books tend to be larger than board books, and they often have red, black and white images as they are much easier for newborn babies to see.

3. **Books with photographs:** Babies are endlessly fascinated with photographs. There are also books that are "touch and feel," meaning the baby can touch and feel the varying texture of images in the book.

4. **Sing-song books**. You could introduce them to books that have a sing-along with repetitive words. They may want to clap along too.

Singing Songs

Speaking of singing, children respond very well when we sing to them or with them. It is often said that music is the universal language. People from all walks of life, backgrounds, cultures, and age groups respond to music, and it's an excellent way to encourage kids to learn and have fun. Combining music and storytelling is powerful. You may want to consider playing a musical instrument or recorded music while reading a book and have the child act out the emotions to the music.

We've looked into how a rich environment will do wonders for children with absorbent minds. Well, part of this richness includes music. It may encourage them to dance or move in some way (which is their motor skills) or sing. It will encourage them to express themselves with confidence, and you may even find they have a gift for music. If you would prefer, you can play a musical instrument as you and your child sing along to songs. You can get really creative and make up lyrics or have them make up words based around a particular theme. You can also sing to them popular nursery rhymes such as "Heads, shoulders, knees and toes." You could even read a book in a sing-along tone.

Singing songs in the form of storytelling will encourage empathy (and wonderful memories).

The Importance of Using Nomenclature

Montessori nomenclature cards are an important way to enhance your child's vocabulary in an easy-to-use and affordable way. Dr. Montessori pioneered these cards to help educate children on the correct names for objects in their environment. Nomenclature is about bringing meaning to something by giving it a name, and since children in their sensitive period are trying to understand the world around them, these cards are a huge benefit to them. The early Montessori nomenclature cards were designed with simple line drawings created by hand because Dr. Montessori believed the child should focus more on the vocabulary and not be distracted by the image.

I suggested earlier that you use "proper" words rather than "baby" words. This is important when using nomenclature so that the child can absorb the vocabulary. Nomenclature cards are also useful if the child hasn't yet started to read. In this situation, you could create (or purchase) cards that contain the image at the top and the name of the picture at the bottom.

You may want to adopt this idea and create your own nomenclature cards rather than purchase them, but that's entirely up to you; there is no right or wrong way.

Listening and Emerging Conversations With Toddlers

Part of the reason a rich language skillset can be developed has to do with the interaction between the educator/parent and the child.

Getting Down on Their Level, Eye-to-Eye Conversations

Kids of all ages dislike when adults speak to them as if they were less smart or use an authoritative manner. That manner includes tone of voice and body language. Rather than speak to the child at full height, which means you have to look down and they look up, why not chat with them on their level, eye to eye. When you do this, the child can better relate to you, and doing so builds trust. It also increases their confidence in their communication skills, encourages them to open up more, and demonstrates the importance of good eye contact. You have an excellent opportunity to put this method into practice when your child is experiencing a tantrum. For instance, rather than scolding them for the tantrum, you could simply make it clear that you acknowledge how they are feeling and that you accept and love them regardless. For example, you could say something like, "You seem upset/frustrated/ hurt/angry. Would you like to show me?" It makes it safe for them to express how they are feeling. When you get into a habit of having eye-to-eye conversations with the child, they will pick up on your "good" habits and will do the same when they are speaking to others. This reflects a child who is equipped with confidence.

Listening and Responding Appropriately

Talk to the child and listen with respect, and you should find they do the same back, as they will unconsciously pick up on your behavior. Here are some useful tips:

- Speak slowly.
- Speak clearly.
- When your child is no longer a baby, try not to speak in "motherese" or using baby talk.
- Bend or crouch down so that you are on the child's level and can speak to him or her eye to eye.
- We often expect our child/children to have manners and be courteous, so we must set an example. Say, "please," "thank you," and "may I?"

- Many people have fallen into the bad habit of waiting to speak rather than simply listening to what the other person has to say. When you are listening to your child, allow yourself to be present, and just listen. You may be surprised to find they do the same.

- Although this guide encourages you to use big words (don't be afraid to, it's how they learn), it's okay at times to say very little and just allow your child to enjoy being held by you or simply focus on whatever catches their attention.

- If your child is reacting inappropriately, you can try speaking quietly and lovingly rather than getting angry. They may grow to understand that reacting out of fear or with anger isn't necessary.

Asking Questions and Respecting Answers

Often, parents can ask questions in a way that leaves the child feeling ashamed or frustrated, and that negativity tends to come from how the question was asked. For example, if the child spills a cup of milk (accidentally or on purpose), your angry or demanding reaction—"Why did you spill your milk??"—can cause the child to react poorly. If you ask the same question in a non-threatening way, you may get a lot further in finding out what's going on with your child. Here are some ways you can ask questions in a way that empowers the child.

1. If you can see that your child is struggling with something, offer to help them. "Would you like any help with putting that back?" "How can I help?" Just give them as much help as they need and then step away.
2. Perhaps you could give them a choice, "Would you like to put on your gloves first or your hat?"
3. Instead of telling your child what to do next, perhaps you could ask them, "What happens next?" This powerful question allows the child to develop independence by getting them to be accountable for their daily life.

41

4. If you are encouraging your child to make something, such as cooking a meal or arts and crafts, it might be a good idea to encourage them by asking what they will need. For example, "What materials do we need?"
5. To help your child express their feelings rather than keep them bottled up, you could ask them, "How do you feel about that?"

Positive Language and Positive Discipline

Against the Word "No"

First of all, cut yourself some slack if you find yourself saying "no" more often than you would prefer. Avoiding "no" with your child can be difficult, especially if you think it's necessary. Many parents struggle with this word because, like you, they want the best for their children, and sometimes they feel the "best" may involve saying "no," depending on what the situation is. First, understand that infants don't really understand what the word "no" means. If your child has picked up an object that is inappropriate, rather than saying "no," simply take it out of their hands and put it out of reach. Alternatively, you can redirect the child to something else if it seems they are about to grasp something they shouldn't.

You may also find it difficult when a child says "no" to you. Again, there are ways around it. Rather than get cross when your child says "no" to you, just change the language. Here are some examples:

You: *"It's time for dinner."*

Child: *"No!"*

You: *"We are going to eat dinner in five minutes. When you have finished playing that game, let's work together to enjoy a delicious dinner."*

Healthy Alternatives and Directed Choice

It's important to use positive language to help build the child's self-confidence. For example, if you tell a child not to drop the glass, it puts the idea in their head that they could drop it, and then they are more likely to (unconsciously). A mother shared with me an incident when her child was enjoying her time on a swing. When the child called out to her mother and said, "Hey mommy, look at me, this is fun," her mother's face dropped, and she called out with a tone of frustration and concern, "Mind you don't fall off!" The child suddenly picked up on her mother's fear of falling off the swing, which in turn caused her muscles to become weak. Her grip loosened, and guess what? She fell off!

It would be a good idea to reframe our language so that it's more positive and empowering. For instance, rather than say, "Don't drop the glass" or "Don't spill the orange juice," perhaps you could say, "Hold the glass with both hands" or "Walk slowly while you're carrying that glass."

Sometimes, a situation may involve some physical redirection, not just with what we say but how we respond to situations. For example, if you can see your child is crawling away from you, it may be tempting to scoop them up. However, perhaps you could stand in front of the child so that you're facing her/him. This may help to redirect the child's movement so it seems like *they are* making the choice to head in a different direction.

If you redirect your child's behavior every time you feel it's appropriate to do so, it teaches them that there are some limits, but does so in a loving and respectful way.

Emotional Learning

Affirming your child's emotions

I have mentioned previously about the importance of accepting children's emotions, even if they are having a tantrum. It may be challenging in the beginning, but over time you may be pleased with the results. If your child is visibly upset, rather than saying, "stop sulking" or "mind your temper," you could instead say something like, "I see you're feeling angry. Why don't you draw how you're feeling... Wow, that's a big circle, you must be feeling so angry." (You'll know instinctively what to say, this is simply a guide).

Mindfulness/Breathing Techniques

Mindfulness is extremely powerful for adults, and the power is even greater in children! Too many people today are living their daily lives in a state of tension, and many times they don't realize it. They are so used to being stressed out that they may believe they're relaxed when they aren't. The slightest change or an unexpected situation may throw somebody who wasn't previously stressed out into a state of anxiety. They may not know how to balance themselves because it generally isn't something people are taught growing up.

If you can help your child to be mindful, you are providing them with an enormous gift that can serve him well into adulthood. Here are some of the benefits for your child:

- Increased social interaction and confidence when communicating with others
- Better focus on tasks
- Improved resilience
- Decreased stress and anxiety
- Encouragement to adopt a more positive attitude towards life
- Improved and regulated emotions—Children are less likely to react to situations.
- Enhanced self-esteem and confidence
- Better health (physical, mental, and emotional) and well-being

Since kids learn so quickly, they will take in information like a sponge. The process of teaching them mindfulness and breathing techniques doesn't need to be long and complicated. Remember the KISS method! Here are some ways you can start to teach mindfulness and breathing techniques to your children:

- Regularly encourage children to think of five things that make them feel happy, that make them smile, or they feel grateful for.

- Get them to breathe in and squeeze all of their muscles so that they have tensed up for a few moments and then let go, taking a deep breath out. This exercise helps to relax the body and breathe out any tension. Lead by example and do the exercise with them (it will relax you too).

- Ask your child to put one or both hands on their heart and feel the heartbeat while taking deep breaths; in through the nose, hold the breath for three seconds, and then slowly exhale through the mouth.

- Walk with your child in nature. Get them to engage their five senses by observing the environment and reporting what they see, hear, feel, and taste. Ask them what textures they feel when they pick up items or touches tree trunks.

- Meditate with your child. Although you will both be silent, it's still a great way to increase the bond between you.

- Whenever your child seems stressed out, just tell them to "stop." Then suggest that they take a few deep breaths and start to observe how they are feeling, what they are thinking, and ask them to breathe out the stress.

- Have positive, uplifting words displayed somewhere in the child's bedroom. That way, upon waking up in the mornings and going to bed at night, your child will see these words of encouragement.

- Where possible, have children take off their shoes and socks. Suggest that they walk around barefoot in the garden while they take deep breaths and observe. This will help them to stay grounded.

Home Activities

There are many things you can do with your child at home, and they can be as simple as arranging flowers. In Montessori classrooms throughout the world, the activities tend to be simple but powerful, and while you're not looking to replicate a classroom, there are some ideas that would work really well in the home setting too. It would be a good idea to expose your child to a variety of activities, but not in a short space of time, as that can be overwhelming. Like with toys, you can choose a couple, and when your child becomes bored, rotate them with other activities. Here are some examples to get you started:

For the Newborn

- Dancing, clapping, and movement in general
- Reading or looking at the pictures in books
- Munari mobile (as previously discussed)
- Finger movement and rhythmic language (poems, songs)
- Musical instruments and musical items, such as a music box
- Grasping objects/toys, even utensils such as a wooden spoon
- Singing lullabies—Babies love this! If this can be performed while they are gently being rocked, all the better.
- Your loving touch—This is essential. Touching newborns with affection will likely put a smile on their faces, and they will feel comforted and loved.

For the Infant

Research shows that a parent's touch helps to develop an infant's brain. A research study at The National University of Singapore presents a first attempt to link early tactile experiences to the developing human brain. The study shows that the frequency of maternal touch, as measured in a 10-minute play session, positively predicts children's resting-state activity in brain regions associated with social functioning. Compared with children receiving less maternal touch, children receiving more maternal touch display greater resting activity and connectivity in the right pSTS. Thus, the present data raise the possibility that, as was shown in the nonhuman brain, tactile care supports emerging social networks in the human brain. (Brauer et al., 2016)

As a Montessori parent, you should consider reading books to your infant as early as possible. Have the child sit on your lap and hold on to them. Doing this encourages bonding between the two of you. You may find that your infant wants to teeth on the book as you are telling the story (common around five or six months old). If you find this occurs, then have a toy handy that you can give for teething instead.

As your child starts to develop their grip, they can participate in the act of reading by turning the pages. This will help increase their focus, and they will probably look forward to getting to the end of a page.

Singing lullabies to your infant will help to increase the bond between you. Even if you don't know any by heart, you can either make something up on the spot or sing a pop song. If you can sing your infant's favorite songs, all the better, as it will further encourage them to join in.

As with a baby, a loving touch with your child is essential to developing self-assurance and self-esteem. Just simply embrace them. Why not give them a kiss and tell them how much you love them? This is bound to lift their spirits. Everyone likes to feel like they matter and are loved, especially at this stage of their development.

For the Toddler

When choosing books for your toddler, there are a few things to take into account:

- It should be a suitable book. Children have different reading needs, so work with what's right for your child, even if a blog post says otherwise.
- You might want to take into account the number of words per page and then ask yourself, "Is this age appropriate?"
- Look for books that are rich in language and contain exciting material.
- Books with real-life images are especially useful. Children want to discover more about the world they are in and their place in

it, so these types of books will help.

Again, as with newborns and infants, toddlers will love it when you sing to them. Observe their reactions, and when you can see that there is a particular song they like, sing it again and have them dance, stamp their feet, and clap their hands with excitement. This will help increase their rhythm and motor skills. Provide a loving touch and encourage them to do the same by getting down on their level and opening up your arms so that they know you want to hug them. You don't even need to express that you want to hug them verbally. Instead, just open your arms and see how they respond.

CHAPTER 4:

MOVEMENT THE MONTESSORI WAY

There is often a lot of emphasis placed on the idea that children should be moving frequently to help keep their weight to a healthy level. However, it isn't just their body weight but also their brain development that should be taken into account when we encourage children to move more. In relation to the Montessori approach, the freedom to move around applies more to them having the opportunity to roam around their classroom and home, both inside and outside.

There is often a sense of irony with how many adults teach children in the traditional style. Parents and teachers want the child to start walking and to be curious as babies, and they encourage this. However, once the child gets to a certain age (still within the sensitive period) where they tend to become curious and want to move around to explore their environment, adults tell them to "sit still." There is often debate as to whether or not a child should sit still. Some experts believe it's essential that children learn to keep still when being taught. For example, The Parent Institute claims, "Children who can't sit still learn that being disruptive gets them attention. They learn to get 'in trouble.' And this can foster long-term discipline problems" (The Parent Institute, 2014). There are many other "experts" who share a similar view about how children should "sit still and learn."

However, is this really necessary? More importantly, does it even work? Surely it leads to more unruly, disruptive behavior in the classroom because it goes against a child's nature. This may not apply to a parent who is struggling with a disruptive child when they are out and about. But when it comes to learning, we must acknowledge that children have a natural inclination to want to move about and explore their environment so that they can learn. Teaching early years children to just "keep still" like robots or lumps of clay seems detrimental to their learning. Dr. Montessori discovered this through her research.

Movement As Essential

Through her research, Dr. Montessori discovered that movement increased a child's ability to learn. In her book, The *Discovery of the Child* (1909), she stated, "One of the most important practical aspects of our method has been to make the training of the muscles enter into the very life of the children so that it is intimately connected with their daily activities." She was very clear throughout her books and lectures that for a child's brain to develop healthily, it was essential that they move their bodies. She also believed that the best form of movement is synthetic movement. This involves moving the body in a way that is intentional and directed towards a particular activity. It's also known as a "knowing activity" as the child's intelligent mind is determining the movement in order for an end goal to be reached.

Dr. Montessori noticed, for example, how children would chase sandpaper letters as they learned sounds. They love to learn by moving around.

The Brain Connection (Learning) With Movement

Dr. Montessori was truly ahead of her time with her observations as she realized that there is a relationship between the brain, senses, and the muscles. She didn't believe that movement was only about improving the heart. Up until recently, almost all educators have thought of movement and the muscular system as aids to respiration, circulation, or as a means for building up physical strength. But in our new conception, the view is taken that movement has great importance in mental development itself, provided that the action which occurs is connected with the mental activity going on." (Montessori, 1949, p. 142)

There is now plenty of research that confirms what Dr. Montessori said over 100 years ago, that there is indeed a connection between brain development and learning. For example, Professor Gabriel Gerry has carried out plenty of research that proves there is a connection between physical activity and brain development. In 2001, he stated that a "growing body of research suggests that physical activity is integral to keeping cognitive processes working on all valves" (Gerry, 2001).

Free Movement and Sensory Exploration

In order for a Montessori child to be able to move around freely in their environment, careful consideration must be applied so that there is some space—even if your home space is confined—and it is safe.

Earlier in this guide, we mentioned the importance of keeping a clean and simple environment. One main reason for this is so the child has the ability to move and explore freely. Everything that exists within the environment ought to be there for a reason and not just for its own sake. To help your child to move around freely and to foster sensory exploration, please consider the following:

- The environment is suitable for the child's height and size.
- Things are reachable for the child. For instance, the shelves are low enough for him to take things off and put them back neatly without any strain.
- Ideally, you want to create an environment that allows the development of the five senses (touch, smell, taste, sound and sight).

- Please remember that while children are given the freedom to move around, they must also be able to abide by certain ground rules in order to develop a respect and appreciation for their environment.
- Don't forget also that free movement and sensory exploration involves being outdoors. It's easy for parents to focus on getting the environment inside the home "just right." Additionally, do make use of being out in nature. This is a powerful way to allow your child to engage their sensory system and move around. It's also free! A trip to the park can be very educational.

Purposeful "Movement" Work

Even today, we still find educators who do not truly grasp the importance and connection between the intellectual mind and moving the physical body. What's profound about Montessori's findings is she discovered that it's *purposeful* movement (movement that's connected to what is being learned), which is the key. For instance, if you ask your child to go and collect ten twigs and bring them back to you, the child is learning to develop muscle memory through an intentional movement.

Integration of Montessori Materials

To encourage the child to be able to integrate Montessori Materials, you could consider sensorial materials three-part cards. They help a child to become familiar with sensory materials and their names. For example, three-part cards contain a "control" card that is printed with a picture of a sensorial image on one side, and on the other side, it states the name of the image. This also has a positive impact on fine and gross motor skills as the child can carry out activities that involve "picture to object" or vice-versa. We will discuss this further shortly.

Benefits of fine and gross motor skills

It's essential to define the difference between fine and gross motor skills. Fine motor skills are what we make to move the small muscles, such as the hands and wrists. So as a parent, you would be looking at how your child holds a pencil, how they use their utensils while they are eating, etc. Gross motor skills are what we use to make movements with all of our muscles, limbs, and joints in a coordinated way. So, when children walk, jump, climb, skip, etc. they are using gross motor skills. Most of the time, gross motor skills relate to their core strength. For example, can they sit up straight? Do they have good control and coordination to run?

Below are some more benefits that fine and gross motor skills can offer your child.

Benefits of fine motor skills

- Children learn to use tools such as scissors, crayons, chalk, pencils, etc. Fine motor skills enable them to cut food, draw, paint, and write, to name a few.
- Children are able to perform essential tasks with more precision, like moving objects, reaching out for things, and grasping. For example, they can zip or button up a coat, write their names or sign them, and turn the pages of their favorite books!
- Hand-eye coordination improves along with fine motor skills. As adults, such coordination allows us to drive cars, wash our hair, etc.
- Children learn to develop their handwriting and draw pictures.
- Children build self-esteem and confidence because they are developing their independence.

Benefits of gross motor skills

- Children are healthy because they can move their bodies through exercise.
- Brain development increases.
- Children release energy through movement.
- A child's self-esteem and confidence increase.

- Children develop the skill of assessing risks, which in turn helps with decision-making as they grow older.

Potty training

You may be asking yourself whether your child is ready to be toilet/potty-trained. Here are some useful tips to help you with this important milestone:

- Bear in mind that it is a natural process and can be gradual. Children tend to be intuitive about what their bodies require, and unconsciously they'll know when they are ready. It will happen at a pace that's right for them and not on parents' schedules. However, you can still encourage them by speaking naturally about their bodies' functions while you are changing their diapers. Remember, their absorbent mind will enable them to take this information in—even as babies!
- You could allow children to play with water in the bathroom sink once they become toddlers since around this time they become fascinated with toilets.
- You may want to have the child sit on a toilet and play a game where he imitates other people in the household.
- Encourage the child to be as independent as possible. Could you find ways to set up your bathroom to allow for this? What about leaving a potty in the bathroom? Could you leave clean clothes or underwear in the bathroom?
- As challenging as it may be, try not to get too emotionally attached. The child will pick up on your emotions, and it can leave them feeling pressured or anxious.
- Don't force a child to use the toilet (or potty).
- Try not to overdo the praise or criticize them.

Overview of Psychomotor Development

Psychomotor development relates to the changes in a child's

cognitive, **communicative**, **physical**, and **socio-emotional** development. These four stages are continuously developing from the moment a child is born, up to their adolescent years.

Infancy (from 0 to 12 months old)

When a child is born, he/she has involuntary reflex movements, which are responses to external stimuli. These movements give a medical expert a good idea of how well brain and nerve development is progressing. For example, a baby will likely hold your finger tightly when you put it in the palm of the baby's hand. This is known as grasp reflex or palmar reflex.

Around two months old, the baby will start to smile at you in response and may also turn their head to follow objects. By the time the baby is three months old, this type of reflex becomes less apparent. The baby's body and muscles are more toned, and they may be able to hold their head firmly for a few moments when you prop them up.

The rooting reflex occurs when you touch the baby's cheek. The baby will turn their head, open their mouth, and suck as if they're being fed. This reflex is needed to help the child feed and it remains throughout infancy. The sucking reflex is similar, except when the roof of the mouth is touched, the baby will begin to suck. The startle, or Moro reflex, allows the child to respond to a sound or noise. They do this by throwing their head back, stretching out their arms and legs, crying, and then again stretching out the arms and legs. This tends to happen quite often until around the age of three to four months old. The tonic neck reflex occurs when the baby's neck is turned to one side, the arm and leg will extend too while the other arm and leg will flex. This takes place up to around three to four months.

At around this age, the baby may reach out for objects and toys, and they may be able to shake an object for a few moments. Between the ages of two to four months old, their vocal cords will start to work. You may find your child starts to laugh hysterically, chirp or babble.

Between four and eight months old, the child will have gained coordination with their movements and will be able to turn their head when someone has called out to them. They will also be able to kick, and their head will likely start to stand straight without the need for someone to prop them up.

Between 12 and 18 months old, your child will be able to stand up and take their first steps forward. However, their stability won't have developed just yet, so they will be prone to bumping into things and falling over. The child will be trying to master their coordination, and you may find them climbing over things, pushing and pulling objects, and crawling around on their hands and knees.

Around 19 to 24 months, the child's motor skills have further developed, and they will be able to go up and down stairs, and even carry a large toy around with them. By the time the child is 24 months, he or she will have mastered climbing the stairs and may possibly be able to ride a tricycle.

Learning Through Play

Playing comes naturally for most children. Even adults want the opportunity to play because it's so fundamental to our nature. It involves *not* setting goals, make-believe, having fun, and enjoying the present moment and spontaneity. Some playful activities have more potential to bring out the best in a child. Here are some examples:

- Playing in the sand. When a child engages in this activity, they are enhancing their scientific learning and physical development. They are scooping up the sand, digging, sifting, and pouring. Essentially, they are finding out more about how things work (sand) and also building their muscles and coordination. If they are playing in the sand with other children, then they are also learning about teamwork, social interaction and the importance of sharing.

- Water play. Similar to sand play, children are learning about the elements and how they work. They get to learn this in a safe environment, and they also get to learn about cause and effect—how there are consequences to actions.

- Roleplay with dressing up. It is fun for children to have the freedom and space to put on dress-up clothes and use props such as "pretend" cooking, doctors and nurses kits, scientist or detective kits. This provides them the opportunity to be anything from a bus driver, singer, shop assistant, fashion designer, inventor, or astronaut. This activity allows the child to start to make sense of the adult world, the roles played out in society, and they start to gain insight into what interests them. Also, when children dress up, it helps to remind them about self-care.

- Playing with dolls or characters. This isn't just about girls playing with dolls. When children are encouraged to play with dolls or mini-figures, such as lego, they are learning about social play, how to label feelings, expression, and of course, imagination.

- Imaginative play helps a child to develop their literacy skills, intellectual reasoning, self-esteem and self-confidence. You only need to leave a child with a few random objects, and they will let their imagination do the rest. This should be encouraged for as long as possible during their childhood years. This will enable them to think outside of the box later in life and also help with their problem-solving skills.

- Nature play. This type of play is healthy, encourages the child to have respect for nature and the environment overall. They also get to learn about biology and their curiosity becomes stimulated. If you let a child out into the great outdoors, their potential to learn and develop will magnify.

Play is one of the best ways a child can learn. Not only does play assist with formal learning later in childhood, but it also encourages scientific thinking. For children who are experiencing early years, play *plays* (pun intended) a pivotal role in childhood development for language, creativity, emotional intelligence and intellectual reasoning.

Play helps a child develop their social, emotional, physical, and intellectual skills. Playtime for the child might involve banging toys around as they stamp their feet, or having two toys play out a scenario that is similar to real life. Children choose to play, and doing so helps with developing their self-esteem because they start to realize what they are capable of doing. They can also develop life skills because often they will imitate the actions and behaviors of adults around them. They also develop their concentration skills due to having so much fun playing that they are completely immersed. If your child is playing with both adults and children, it will help them to become socially confident as they grow older.

Here are some ways your child can develop motor skills through playing:

- Physically playing by running, throwing, peddling, rolling around, and climbing. These activities will help with gross motor skills.
- To encourage your child to grow their fine motor skills, why not let them button up their shirt or zip up their coat? Writing is excellent for encouraging children to put down their thoughts and feelings in the written word; it will do wonders for them. If they are able to write, perhaps they could start to write down things they are grateful for daily. This also encourages positivity and happiness.

Home Activities

For the Newborn

- Give your newborn containers to play with
- Play peek-a-boo with your baby
- Hide and seek
- Play music and clap
- Read books

- Let them see themselves in the mirror

For the Infant

- Three-colored spheres (previously discussed)
- Dancing and singing
- Object performance using sensorial materials such as three-part cards
- Interlocking rings—This involves three or four rings that are interlocked. This is an excellent grasping toy.
- They could stick and separate hair rollers
- Play with stickers and felt
- Stack toy utensils; stack and knock over (empty) cups
- DIY finger paints
- Play with giant felt pieces
- Pincer grip: pull fabric pieces from a tissue box

For the Toddler

- Helping out when you're washing up—If you make this fun, they'll get into the habit of doing this even as they grow older.
- Singing and playing musical instruments
- Playing ball games
- Weaving and sewing
- Walking heel to toe on a line—an excellent way to enhance motor skills and focus
- Playing with dough, painting pictures and drawing—These activities are still fun even for adults!
- Playing make-believe or "let's pretend"
- Building blocks—especially Lego!
- Playing with sand and water—This activity will allow the child to understand that water isn't solid.

CHAPTER 5:

FEEDING THE MONTESSORI WAY

We want our children to receive the best start in life, and that includes a healthy balanced diet. The Montessori way takes into account the importance of nutrition together with how your child is being fed. Many people take for granted the idea that eating a healthy diet alone isn't always enough; the environment in which we feed our bodies can play a huge role in our health. For instance, if you are feeling *rushed* and trying to eat your lunch, even if you have a plate full of vegetables, is it really good for your health? If you are eating your healthy cooked evening meal but your immediate surroundings consist of angry shouting, dust and chemicals from construction, or an alarm bell going off, how good can that really be for your nervous and digestive systems? Each one of these things alone causes the body to feel stressed, and if you are consuming food while this type of chaos is taking place around you, it may not be beneficial for your health. This certainly applies to when children are being nourished.

Breastfeeding and the Baby-Mother Bond

There is much debate in the world about breastfeeding. Some people feel ready to stop after two or three months, and other parents are adamant that a child should be breastfed until they are at least two years old. No one can say what is right for you and your baby's body. I would strongly advise that you ultimately tune into your baby's unique needs as well as your own. However, this section aims to give you a guideline as to what the recommendations are and how to feed using the Montessori approach.

According to the World Health Organization in 2019, "Exclusive breastfeeding is recommended up to 6 months of age, with continued breastfeeding along with appropriate complementary foods up to two years of age or beyond (World Health Organization). You may find that breastfeeding isn't an option for you. That's fine. It's important that you do things based on your own personal preferences and situation. Here are some tips on how to get the most out of feeding your newborn baby, whether that be through breastfeeding or bottle feeding. Feeding your newborn baby is a fantastic opportunity to develop a strong bond, and I encourage you to make the most of it.

Ideally, try and find a quiet place (peaceful, too, if possible) where you can sit and feed your baby without being distracted. If our adult bodies get stressed out when we are eating somewhere that's busy and loud, imagine the impact on the newborn! Please remember, it's highly recommended that you *don't* get involved in other activities while you are breastfeeding. The Montessori approach recognizes the importance of the parent tuning into the baby's needs.

If you breastfeed, you may find that you naturally change sides. If you are bottle-feeding, then remember to switch sides so that your newborn's body has the chance to work on developing gross motor skills and eye-to-eye contact with you. The eye-to-eye contact will, of course, help to increase the baby-mother bond.

Child-Led Weaning

Beginning at Six Months

Weaning is the process your baby goes through by transitioning from the milk your body produces to consuming foods from other sources. For example, it could be the transition from a baby drinking his mother's breast milk to eating pureed food or solids. Depending on the child's needs, this can take some adjustment and often requires the parent to be patient. The Montessori approach advises weaning the child between four to six months. Generally, many parents feel ready to start their child weaning from six months onwards. Again, it is important that you follow your own intuition and also observe the cues on when your child is ready to move to solid foods.

Here are some indicators that your child may be ready to start weaning:

- Your baby appears to be interested in food.
- Your baby can sit up or roll over.
- Your baby is now able to support his or her own head weight.
- Teething has started.
- Your baby is able to control their hands well.

Since there is so much information on whether you "should" or "should not" wean and when to start, you may feel a little unsure. To help you gain more clarity, here are some pros and cons of baby-led weaning. Consider them carefully and then go with what's right for your child:

Pros

- Since babies are curious, if you baby-led wean, they will have the opportunity to pick up their food and explore, which will develop their independence.
- Your baby will get used to different types of food, their tastes, textures, smells. It will help them to accept food better. Sometimes when children are given a limited range of food, they can become fussy.
- The baby can be offered or receive the same type of food as

the rest of the household which helps to increase their social skills.

- Perhaps a baby is less likely to overeat if they are the ones feeding themselves. They eat at their own pace and can decide what they want to eat.

Cons

- It can be messier because your baby is bound to get food on the table, floor, or all over their face and clothes.
- Some parents worry about choking, but as long as your baby is sitting upright, they will be fine.

No Use of High Chairs

The Montessori approach avoids the use of high chairs when it comes to weaning, as it goes against the philosophy of children being given child-size, comfortable furniture that allows them to move around independently. The Montessori weaning table and chair foster independence and freedom of movement. In addition, it gives the baby a place (and space) of their own to sit down and enjoy their meal in the way they observe their parents doing. It gives the child a sense of achievement and belonging and will also help to develop table manners. It's best to ensure the table you provide for your child is strong and sturdy so that the child can move in and out without the risk of it tipping over.

Child-Size Dishes, Utensils, and Natural Materials

As with furniture, careful consideration must be given when providing children with the appropriate tools for whatever tasks they are to perform. In this case, it's feeding. If the utensils and plates are too big, it will be far too difficult for them to feed themselves properly, which will leave them frustrated. It is important to purchase child-sized plates and utensils so they can nourish themselves comfortably and further develop their coordination and motor skills. The Montessori approach recommends you provide your child with tools, utensils, cloths, and dishes made from natural materials for feeding time. Natural materials include tempered glass (they are less likely to break), real wood, cotton, and metal.

Involving the Child in Food Preparation

Since we know that children love to learn and explore their environments naturally, helping to prepare the food and table will leave them feeling satisfied with their achievements. In the Montessori classroom, children are encouraged to prepare, set, clear, and clean up after themselves. This is an activity that can be replicated at home to provide them with practical life skills. Why not suggest that they help to set the table, clear it, and clean up once they have finished eating? Doing this will help to bring on a healthy daily habit, a learned behavior that will serve them well into adulthood. Here are some suggestions:

- Peel fruit and vegetables
- Wash dishes
- Set table
- Clear the table
- Clean up properly

Be prepared; things will get messy!

Learning Table Manners

It is important to set an example when it comes to setting the table, as your child will copy you. There is no use expecting the child to set the table up in a certain way when you aren't doing that yourself. Once you start to allow your child to sit at a weaning table and encourage them to help with food preparations, you may find that they will begin to learn table manners. What table manners are you teaching your children? Here are some examples:

- How to set the table properly

- How to hold utensils properly
- How to hold "breakable" items correctly (holding a glass with two hands)
- How to clear the table after dinner
- How to clean the dining area, utensils and dishes
- How to store things away correctly
- How to say "please," "thank you," "may I," "excuse me," etc.
- Chewing with mouth closed

What are other table manners that are important in your household?

Setting the Table

To help your child set the table in a way that doesn't cause too much chaos, such as glasses smashing and food landing everywhere other than on the plate, it's important for the child to understand that setting the table one piece at a time is ideal. First, it allows the child to focus on that particular task and work on the required motor skills. Second, it prevents the child from getting overwhelmed, and third, it will be *slightly* less messy! Eventually, when children have mastered this, they can set the table with two pieces at a time.

The Importance of a Child Cleaning Up

If children learn from an early age about the importance of cleaning up after themselves, it may prevent a lot of frustration for parents further down the line. The Montessori approach encourages children to foster independence and responsibility by understanding the importance of cleaning up their messes when they have finished. In addition, it teaches children to respect their environments, and they come to appreciate that a task (cooking, eating or playing) isn't just about actually *doing* the task, but also includes the preparation beforehand and cleaning up afterwards.

Having children clean up after themselves and contribute to cleaning up for the rest of the household can become a fun activity. If it feels like a chore to them, they are more likely to complain or throw a tantrum. However, if you can find ways to get creative and make it fun, it will be exciting for all of you!

Home Activities

For the Newborn

- Sing to them while breastfeeding or bottle-feeding.
- Rock gently with them while breastfeeding.
- Make sure to use eye contact with your child during feeding.
- Let the child pick up food, such as a small piece of cooked broccoli, and allow them to work with that.
- Encourage the child by smiling and clapping as they put the food into their mouths.

For the Infant

- **Finger food**—To help the child transition into eating solids, perhaps you could let them use their fingers first. They will likely find this to be fun.
- **Read stories** about boys and girls weaning and/or eating solids.
- **Food play**—Encourage your child to crush a variety of different textured food you lay out for them (berries, crackers, etc.).
- **Hide food**—Since infants love to play hide and seek, play a hidden treasure game where you chop up small pieces of food (fruit and vegetables) and hide them in a bowl someplace where the child won't have difficulty finding it.
- **Toy tea party or teddy bear picnic**—Why not have a tea party with their favorite toys or go on a picnic with their favorite teddy bear? Bring yours too!
- **Wild food foraging**—Let them help you pick edible herbs,

fruits, or vegetables that can be prepared for dinner.

For the Toddler

- Read stories with them about food preparation and weaning.
- Provide instruction about and practice washing foods.
- Allow them to help with cooking or baking.
- Create food with faces using bananas, apples, and oranges, and decorate them with eyes, nose, and mouth (using currants, berries, and whatever else they want).
- Play a game where you put different types of food down in front of the child with the child's eyes closed. The child then has to guess the food that's in front of him through touch, smell, or taste.
- Work together to chop up food.
- Allow him to dress up and play the role of chef, baker, or waiter/waitress.
- Have them peel a hard-boiled egg.

CHAPTER 6:

EXPLORATION THE MONTESSORI WAY

Exploration is an essential aspect of the Montessori Way, and it includes indoor exploration as well as outside. Dr. Montessori advised that the environment must stimulate and promote interest in the child. In relation to outdoor exploration, there may be questions firing in your head, such as, is it safe? What about the weather? What about supervision? What if the child refuses to come inside no matter what? What if he puts something in his mouth that he shouldn't? The list goes on. Don't worry, there are ways that the child can explore safely and freely. What's important is that the child is provided with a cozy home environment.

When you think of how you are going to set up the indoors of your home environment according to Montessori principles, remember to consider how it's going to benefit your child. Furniture should fit the child's body and equipment should be lifelike.

Exploring Safely and Freely

For indoor exploration, we have previously looked at how the indoor environment can be set up to allow your child to have free movement. The first step we discussed is to ensure the rooms are childproof, and this may involve you getting down on your hands and knees to see things from your child's point of view.

The Importance of a Safe and Clutter-Free Environment

Less is more! Having less clutter in the house will help to stimulate your child's imagination because it gives them the opportunity to play "make-believe." When children are overwhelmed with so much stuff, they can become overstimulated, easily bored, or their attention is drawn to the next item or object, and they are less likely to rely on their imagination. In addition, having a cluttered environment (inside and outside) can be dangerous. They may trip—or you might!

When you keep the home safe and tidy, children will learn a few things. First, they will learn that everything belongs in a certain place, and items should be stored away neatly when they have finished with them.

Another important lesson that comes from being responsible for putting items away is that more items require more work. This helps demonstrate the value of living within one's means. It's not necessary to consume so much just for the sake of consuming. Often, the happiest people in the world are those who appreciate and value what they have, not those who demand more and more and are still never satisfied.

While children can learn to value a few things highly, they can also come to appreciate that freedom that comes with discarding old or broken items. Everything has a purpose, and when toys, clothes, or other objects can no longer fulfill their purposes, they just become clutter and need to be removed.

Lastly, a clutter-free environment helps communicate the value for shared space and for the environment itself. Putting things away is a means of caring and respecting those items as well as the environment.

Creating a safe environment isn't just about keeping it clutter-free and childproof; it should also evoke a feeling of safety and comfort within the child. Here are some ideas for how you can create an environment that leaves your child feeling genuinely safe and reassured:

- Natural wood furniture
- An indoor water feature that is quiet
- Fresh flowers and plants
- Artwork—Maria Montessori suggested depictions of children or children and mothers. Fathers are great, too!
- Open space for the child to move around easily
- Living plants and animals
- Photos/portraits of peace activists such as Dr. Montessori and Gandhi
- Objects or images that are related to peace, love, compassion, and friendship
- The environment should be warm

Don't Do Anything for Them!

There is a Montessori motto, "help me do it myself." Allow children to build their independence and figure things out on their own unless you see they are really struggling. If they do seem like they need assistance, ask if they would like help with their chosen activity. If you have set up the indoor environment so that it's clutter-free and safe, there shouldn't be any major issues with them moving around freely to discover their independence.

Resist the Urge To Plan Their Day

Just because the Montessori approach doesn't encourage planning a child's day, the day needn't be chaotic, disorganized, and scattered. Far from it. In a Montessori environment, the child is given the opportunity to learn time management skills so that they can self-regulate their daily life effectively. Their time management skills will develop if we set up the right kind of environment to start with. Your child will be carrying out practical life activities, and this alone will help them to be efficient and act in a timely manner.

Let Babies/Toddlers Be on the Floor With Free Range of Movement

Just allow them to explore being on the floor without feeling like you should intervene. Simply follow them and observe. When babies and toddlers move around, they are learning about coordination. Even when they fall down, they are still learning. The more they move, the more they develop control of their movements. You may find it tempting to scoop them up or prevent them from going somewhere. Unless they are crawling or moving towards something dangerous (which shouldn't be the case if they are in a room that's been childproofed), simply let them be.

Dr. Montessori's "Practical Life Activities"

Dr. Montessori cleverly devised a term called "practical life activities," which are about the tasks the child experiences in daily life and connect to all areas of their life. These activities tend to be related to the child's culture and it helps them to feel as if they belong.

Practical life activities are based around four key components: **Grace and courtesy, caring for the environment, caring for the self**, and the **movement of objects**.

Practical life activities are learned quickly by the child and this includes practical life activities they observe from adults around them. A really good way of assisting your child to develop their practical life activities is to allow them to be around when you carry out everyday activities. When you do this, the child starts to feel valuable and grows in self-esteem. He will also learn to trust his environment, and since he has seen his parent(s) carry out particular activities, it will encourage him to do the same.

Real-Life, Day-to-Day Activities

The following gives an idea of what real-life, day-to-day activities consist of:

1. Not restrictive
2. Self-contained
3. Reality-based
4. Cultural
5. Safety
6. Ideally, only one of each activity—This helps the child to develop patience and perseverance.
7. Completed—The child must understand that the activity should be finished, otherwise they may fall into the habit of constantly starting something and never finishing it.

We have spoken of a number of real-life, day-to-day activities already. However, here are some examples of practical life activities that your child may benefit from doing:

1. Buckling shoes or tying shoelaces
2. Making fruit juice
3. Watering plants and flowers
4. Hanging up clothes to dry (there are child-sized clothes pegs)
5. Polishing shoes
6. Help sibling/s with chores around the house
7. Cleaning the inside part of the windows
8. Self-care, including blowing their nose with a tissue or handkerchief
9. Helping to create or wrap gifts for birthdays or Christmas, etc.

More Ideas

There are plenty of things the child can carry out in the kitchen or dining area. Quite a few have been mentioned, but there is still plenty more:

- Serving the rest of the household dinner and clearing away their plates. However, if you find that your child is struggling to pick up larger plates, then have him stick to the smaller ones, such as side plates, drinking cups/glasses, and utensils.

- When your child is working with utensils and dishes that are suitable for their size, they feel comfortable and, at the same time, responsible and successful because they have been able to model the adults (or older siblings).
- When the kitchen activities are looked upon as being fun rather than chores, you will have a much easier time getting them to help out.
- Open and close lids (including dustbin lids)
- Wash their hands, body, and face
- Brush their teeth—properly
- Wash fruits and vegetables
- Set out napkins, plates, and utensils properly

Age-Appropriate Chores

1 to 1½ years

- Get dressed (with assistance)
- Peel and chop a banana
- Take plate into the kitchen
- Take cup into the kitchen
- Brush teeth properly (with assistance)
- Brush hair
- Fetch shoes
- Help to pack away shoes
- Pack away toys
- Fetch diaper or underwear
- Turn the light switch on/off
- Wash hands
- Drink from a glass (not a glass that's full)

- Pour a glass/jug of fruit juice or milk using a toddler-size jug
- Help prepare breakfast - put cereal into a bowl and pour on milk

1½ to 3 years

- Prepare a light snack
- Choose clothes to wear
- Get dressed with minimal effort (if any)
- Clean windows
- Water plants and flowers
- Brush the pet/s
- Put the leash on the dog
- Brush teeth properly
- Clean face and wash body
- Fetch cup and saucer
- Dust furniture
- Help unpack groceries
- Put toys and objects back on shelves, in baskets, or in storage boxes
- Help to load and unload the washing machine or dishwasher
- Sweep floor
- Wipe the table
- Pack a bag and carry it
- Sweeping
- Wiping table

The Role of a Parent As an Effective Modeler

Other than being a guide for your child, you are also a modeler because children like to emulate their parents or the adults who are important in their lives. Although the saying, "actions speak louder than words" is cliché, it is also very true. If you are looking to be an effective modeler, it's important that you set an example with your actions. Your child will be observing how you behave and they will try to be the same way (consciously and unconsciously, although at this stage, they are mainly operating from the unconscious). A question to ask yourself sometimes is, "Would I want my child to behave the way I am right now?" If the answer is "no," then it is your responsibility to do something about it.

Dr. Maria Montessori realized that children naturally copy adults, and so quite a number of Montessori methods are done without the use of words. Again, it comes down to the child wanting to explore the environment and to understand their identity better. You can really get creative and have some fun with this. At the same time, it's a chance for you to stop some bad habits. For instance, if you have a habit of texting while you're driving or crossing the road, be aware. The chances are that when your child is learning to drive or is old enough to cross the street on their own, they are likely to copy your habits—which could be dangerous.

Exploring Outside the Home

In a world where most people are glued to their electronic devices, including children, it's a beautiful gift to be able to provide your child with nature. It is strongly advised that you don't introduce electronic devices or technology into their lives too early. Ideally, not before the age of four. If your child was to attend a traditional school, then it cannot be helped. However, for as long as you are able to, in your Montessori home, try to redirect their attention away from cell phones and other devices.

If, when thinking about leading your child outdoors, you are concerned about the weather, then the best solution is to make sure your child is dressed suitably for it. For instance, if it's snowing, make sure they are wearing protective layers and boots with a strong grip. In Norway, people believe that bad weather doesn't exist; it's more about how you are dressed that can be considered "bad," so you must wrap up sensibly.

We spoke earlier about carefully inspecting each room in the house and childproofing them. It's a good idea to also check your garden (if you have one) or where possible, the area around your home to make sure it is safe. Do you have any furniture stacked outside that could topple over with the right nudge? Is there any wood with nails poking out? Are there any cracks or heaves in the concrete that could cause someone to trip?

Nature is a second Montessori space

Once you have decluttered and inspected outside, getting value from time outside is pretty simple because you can rely on the materials provided by nature to educate and stimulate your child. Please remember that the materials offered by nature are as intriguing (if not more) to children as the ones indoors.

Children can take their mats or tables and chairs outside to perform certain activities. For instance, if they have comfy chairs, they may want to sit outside and read or paint. Alternatively, they can sit on the grass or under a tree for some quiet reading or meditation.

Your child can gain some fantastic practical life skills by spending time outside in nature. For instance, they can rake the lawn (child-size rake), sweep up the leaves, and plant fruits and vegetables. Planting healthy food in the garden will do wonders because, in addition to the other benefits, it will encourage the child to eat healthy.

A sandbox and free play are great ways to allow your child to have fun and learn without having anything planned. As they spend time playing in the sandbox, your child is exploring the texture of sand and making shapes, including castles. This is a great way to develop fine motor skills. Children can also write their names and other words in the sand. If they decide to bury themselves in the sand, they get a sense of their body as it relates to space.

Home Activities

For the Newborn

- Allow the infant to crawl around outside and be fascinated with nature
- Talk to neighbors
- Watch people go by and be fascinated
- Scrunch up the leaves
- Listen to animals that are close by
- Play with balls outside
- Play musical instruments
- Take playdough or plasticine outside
- Take music outside and dance to it

For the Infant

- Do some weeding
- Clean the outside windows.
- Plant flowers and plants
- Help to create garden features such as plant pots with faces
- Playgrounds
- Water play
- Play in the sand
- Practice walking

For the Toddler

- Landscaping and gardening
- Nature walks
- Meditation and mindfulness
- Treasure hunt
- Collect items
- Spot different animals, plants, and flowers
- Treasure hunt games
- Going to the park
- Visiting the zoo

- Going swimming

Reading: Intellectual Exploration

One way to encourage your child to read is to create a reading corner somewhere in the home. If you provide a very comfortable seat, such as a soft couch (child-size), the child is more likely to find reading time to be fun. Here are some simple steps to create an appropriate reading nook:

1. Have shelves that are accessible. If you use adult bookshelves, then the child won't be able to reach the books. Or if they try to, it could put their safety at risk. When you provide child-size shelves, the child can access the book and then put it back neatly without any fuss.

2. The furniture doesn't need to be expensive. You can make a piece yourself or simply use a basket or wooden crate that is tucked away neatly in the room. The child will see this as her library or reading corner.

3. It's important to make the reading nook cozy, so a comfortable child-size chair or couch is one option. You could even opt for a floor mat, a few pillows, or you could place a rug down to help define the area.

4. Please remember to decorate the area with small details that matter! It could be a funky lamp, family portrait, the child's favorite toy, a beautiful piece of artwork, or a plant. The list of what you might want to choose is virtually endless.

CHAPTER 7:

SOCIALIZING THE MONTESSORI WAY

Although the Montessori Method emphasizes the importance of a child learning to be independent, the child must also know how to work well with others and interact with confidence. Strong social skills are encouraged from birth. Dr. Montessori herself said that "…we must begin our work by preparing the child for the forms of social life, and we must attract his attention to these forms." (The Montessori Method, 1909).

Children under the age of six years old often prefer to work alone because they are discovering their identity. However, it's still important that they are encouraged to develop their social skills on a daily basis.

The Basis of Socialization

The basis of socialization is a strong bond with a loving caregiver. It's essential that you perceive caregiving as bonding. Although certain caregiving tasks, such as changing diapers and feeding, can seem exhausting, they are an opportunity to build the relationship between you and your baby. The Montessori approach encourages the caregiver to see these moments as a chance to connect and deepen the bond with your baby. If your baby has a strong bond with a loving caregiver, it will provide them with safety and comfort. This is likely to instill confidence and trust in themselves and their caregivers. They will know that they are valued and cared for no matter what, which then frees them up to focus on learning about their environment and finding out more about their identity. Also, if the child is fully aware that he or she is valued and free to express themselves, they will confidently express their thoughts and feelings in social settings because they know they are loved and taken care of regardless. That sense of security is vital for social interaction.

Interactions With Parent/Caregiver

Although many parents wait until the child is a year or older before they encourage social interactions with others, you can start children off from day one. For instance, when the child is born, they can be encouraged to develop their social skills through interactions with the parent or caregiver. Earlier in the guide, we discussed the importance of maintaining eye contact with children, even when they are babies and are being bottle-fed or breastfed. Don't underestimate the power of communication; it's still important to talk to them. Emphasize how much you love them.

Every day, build on the bond between you and your child by listening to them. Don't just talk over your child or tell them to shut up. If you're critical of a child when they are reaching out to you for help, you may cause them to shut down or lose trust in you. If a child did not receive a strong bond with a loving caregiver, it could leave them feeling like they have not been able to figure out their identity. In turn, they may experience social anxiety later in life or try to shape themselves so that they are like a certain person they admire.

If you can offer your child a loving relationship and your child responds well, then the child's social skills will flourish.

The bond between caregiver and child is a two-way process. It is interactive, and sometimes it's easy for caregivers to forget this. To help encourage interaction with babies and infants, you can narrate what you are doing. For example, if you are changing a diaper, tell the child exactly what you are doing and why. Remember to smile and use eye contact. When you communicate clearly and respectfully to your child, they will likely do the same because they will be mimicking you. Talk with your child and narrate activities to keep them engaged. If they are a little older, perhaps you could ask them to crawl towards the clean diapers or point to them.

Another principle to consider from the two-way nature of your interaction with children is that they are people in their own rights. This is true even for infants. They still need you to act as a guide to them, but they need your respect like they need your guidance. Don't make assumptions about what you think they are capable of or not, as this will leave them feeling discouraged.

An effective way to demonstrate that you see children as their own persons is to give them freedom of movement in their environment. For a newborn, this includes not holding them for long periods or keeping them somewhere that is restrained or too confined, such as in a stroller, carrier, or similar devices. Also, allow your baby to crawl around without feeling the need to scoop them up (unless they are heading somewhere that could cause a risk to their well-being). Give them time to simply look around the room or at objects, in awe and wonder.

To help increase the bond between you and your child, you could smile at them, and playing peek-a-boo is a great way. It's also important that you respond to children's cues. For instance, if they are laughing, acknowledge their laughter and copy them. If they turn their heads to look at something, again, make it clear to them that their reactions have been noted and respond accordingly. If they suddenly look surprised or smile, copy them by looking surprised. When you respond to babies' cues, you encourage them to keep responding and reacting to their environment. This builds trust because they know on some level that they are being heard and noticed and that you value their expressions and input.

Learning Socialization Through Play

Children love to play. It's natural for them. We also know that children love to learn. When they play, they are learning. At some point, people (adults) decided that play and learning are two separate activities. Do you notice how children often don't learn as well if what they are being taught isn't fun or engaging? If they find it boring, they will switch off, become distracted, or get frustrated. In order to teach them to socialize, you can do these in a fun way—through play. It will also help them to be more confident in social settings later, and they are more likely to perceive socializing as being fun even as adults.

One on One With Caregiver

During the times you are having one-on-one moments with your child, it's a good idea for you not to have your phone with you or spend most of the time engaged in other amusements. Your child will feel like he/she isn't worth your time as much as whoever is on the other end of the cell phone. They might think that they are boring or not interesting enough to keep your attention. This belief can leave them feeling they are just not interesting or engaging enough, and they might withdraw or experience social anxiety further down the line.

Research shows that when children play with their parents, it enhances their self-esteem and self-image because they feel special. Children are looking for praise and attention. They want to know that they are approved of and belong to the family or a group. When you spend valuable time with your child, they appreciate it (well into adulthood).

You need this one-on-one time to be present with your child and attentive to their needs. Not only will this help the child, but you will also feel a sense of satisfaction and achievement. It's a chance to connect with your own inner-child too.

Side-by-Side Play

Since children are generally looking to discover their identities for the first few years of their lives, they tend to play independently. However, you may find that they start to play side by side. They could even be playing the same game or with the same toy as they sit or stand next to each other, but they aren't playing with each other. This is also known as "parallel play." "Associate play" is similar, except the children are working on their own activities or projects. This type of play introduces team building, and communication skills will be developed. Eventually, around four or five years old, they will be ready to play together, which will give them a chance to build their collaborative skills.

Teaching Grace and Courtesy

Dr. Montessori recognized the importance of children needing order on some deeper level. As a Montessori parent, you will need to give the child space and freedom to discover themselves, and this will be done by creating order in the household. So, as a parent, it's essential to recognize that there needs to be a balance. This will help your child to develop the skills of manners, kindness, consideration, and being caring towards oneself and others. Teaching children about grace and courtesy helps them to find their identity.

Learning Social Structures and How To Interact in Activities

Toddlers tend to be naturally empathetic. For instance, they become concerned or want to help when a baby is crying or an animal is in distress. They seem to have a strong urge to help or serve in some way. This is because they recognize the same feeling or emotion within themselves, and that helps them to understand their identity further. As a result, they can show a deep understanding or compassion towards others and in situations.

A child's sensitive period is an ideal time to learn about grace and courtesy. These ideas will help the child to develop cultural awareness so that they can understand how to act and behave accordingly. This will also encourage them to have respect for themselves as well as others.

Some of the things a child learns in the Montessori environment through grace and courtesy include:

- Offering food
- Knowing when to say "please" and "thank you"
- Compassion and kindness
- Patience
- Knowing how and when to shake hands
- Knowing when to apologize and excuse oneself
- Understanding not to interrupt and knowing when to ask for help
- Using a quiet tone of voice where and when it's necessary
- Taking turns and sharing
- Blowing one's nose
- Covering one's mouth when coughing or sneezing
- Respecting other people's space and boundaries
- Washing one's hands
- Cleaning and tidying up after oneself
- Introducing oneself
- Knowing when to be silent
- Speaking politely
- Caring for their environment (indoors and outdoors)
- Making friends
- Carrying objects/items

Saying "Please and Thank You"

Although this was mentioned on the list above, it's important to reiterate the importance of children learning to say "please" and "thank you." Your child will go much further in daily life, and the relationships they build will be stronger if they understand the importance of saying these words. It teaches them the importance of being kind, appreciative, and respectful of what they receive or expect. It will also enable them to make friends and participate in teamwork.

The Montessori approach recognizes that a child naturally has the desire to be gracious and courteous. Therefore a gentle approach to encouraging them should do wonders for their behavior and characteristics. Remember, when *you* say "please" and "thank you," they will copy you. When you give your child something or ask for something, be sure to tell them "please" and "thank you." Eventually, there will come a point when they will automatically know to say it themselves.

How To Walk and Sit

Part of a child's education on grace and courtesy involves how they move their body, especially when walking and sitting. In a Montessori classroom, the child may learn how to walk around a rug, for instance. This is something you can replicate at home. Here's an example:

Get a rug, unfold it, and put it in your home. Then ask your child to watch as you walk around the rug carefully, ensuring you don't cut any corners. Ask your child to follow or repeat what you did. When they complete this task successfully, you can inform them that they now know how to walk around a rug.

This little exercise will help them to walk safely, calmly, and with awareness. Tripping over a rug is a common thing for children (and adults), but you may help eliminate that risk or reduce it significantly by teaching your child how to walk with care. You can help your child to sit upright so that they have good posture by having them sit in a chair that encourages them to sit straight. They can practice sitting correctly and not fidgeting too much while they are at the dinner table.

Opportunities for Socialization

To help children make the most of socializing with other people, observe their social strength/s, and encourage them to use them. For example, is your child able to think creatively? Do they have a good sense of humor? Are they good at listening? If so, how could you get them to develop this skill further? Is your child excellent at speaking? Do they speak with clarity and politeness? Again, can you encourage them to use these skills in a social setting, and if so, how? Also, focus on social traits that are not so strong in your child. For example, is your child a fantastic listener but doesn't really give eye contact? Is your child verbally expressive, but does he/she interrupt other people? The goal here is not to be critical but to instead compliment the child on their strengths and then find ways you can encourage them to hone their skills or improve on the ones they are not so strong in.

Here are several developmentally appropriate ways to enhance the socializing skills of your child.

For the Newborn

- Make eye contact and smile at them.
- Talk to them and give a commentary on everything you are doing and why (such as changing their diaper).
- Sing to them.
- Copy them.
- Attend social gatherings where other newborns will be present so that they can interact with each other.
- Take your newborn on different trips to places like the zoo, the park, baby parties, family gatherings, outdoor events, the library, etc.
- Encourage family members and friends to hold the baby if they feel comfortable doing so.
- Babble and talk to your baby, but make sure you pause so that they can react, and then respond to their reaction with facial expressions and words.

For the Infant

- Take them to storytime at the library.
- Schedule playdates or meetups with other parents and their children.
- Have playdates that involve just you and your child.
- Visit places where they can have fun and learn, such as a museum.
- Involve the child in daily errands, such as shopping.
- Take them to the theater.
- Allow them to spend time with other children (supervised).
- Go for picnics.

For the Toddler

- Schedule playdates or meetups with other parents and their children.
- Have playdates that involve just you and your child.
- Have pretend tea parties.
- Have real tea parties.
- Tell jokes and encourage them to do so.
- Play charades.
- Look for child-friendly events or activities in your area.
- Allow them to spend time with other children (supervised).
- Allow them to spend time with people from different age ranges.
- Allow them to spend time with adults you know well outside of the family.
- Tell them about the social skills you want them to know. For instance, if they have a toy or game, give it to them and say, "I am handing you this toy because it is good to share."
- Encourage them to socialize with family and friends. For example, "Come and say 'hello' to Auntie Jenny."

- Go to storytime at the library.

CHAPTER 8:

SENSITIVE PERIOD

We briefly looked at what the sensitive period is in chapter one of this guide. Now it's time to delve deeper into this essential stage of a child's life.

Sometimes a sensitive period is so obvious that even if someone hasn't studied the Montessori approach, they will be aware of the period. An example is a child learning to walk between one year and one and a half years old. Sometimes, though, the sensitive period may not be so obvious and will require more observation and intuitive insight for the adult. For example, a two-year-old may be having what many refer to as "terrible twos" or a series of temper tantrums, when in reality the child is looking to learn about order in their environment. As a parent, if you can nurture this sensitive period and provide the type of environment that will enable the infant or toddler to learn what they need, it will assist them greatly.

What Is a Sensitive Period?

Dr. Montessori recognized that there were certain times in a child's early years that appeared to be more sensitive to them than at any other time. She referred to them as "sensitive periods." These are stages when a child can more easily learn about specific ideas, skills, or traits. The child will show a strong interest in certain activities or might demonstrate aversion for others. Essentially, sensitive periods are times when a child concentrates on one specific object or stage of development. Dr. Montessori once said, "It is this sensibility [sensitive periods] which enables a child to come into contact with the external world in a particularly intense manner. Every effort marks an increase in power" (1949).

A Review and Discussion of Each Sensitive Period

Small Objects

Children in this sensitive period become obsessed with small objects and fine details. Around one year old, the child will begin to be more independent with their movement, and the environment will appear larger, giving them the urge to explore. This is normally a sign that the child is starting to understand order and detail more. The child will likely be fascinated with pebbles, stones, insects, and glass. You may find that your child tries to put these objects into their mouth. Since they are seeking to understand the outer world, they have a natural urge to pay attention to detail.

To help the child prepare for this stage, it is a good idea for you to ensure you have childproofed the environment (by getting down on your hands and knees, as previously mentioned).

Movement

From birth to one year, your child is trying to improve their coordination skills. They will try to perfect their movement through practice, and you may find that they are constantly looking to wander around. Movements they will practice and seek to perfect include grasping, walking, touching, balancing, crawling, and turning. Your role in this practice should be a casual observer or supporter. For example, when your child is learning to walk, you may have the urge to take your child by the hand and walk around at your pace. But that's not beneficial for the child's development. Doing so will likely leave the child frustrated and tired. Then you'll be left to carry them around! Instead, try walking at the child's pace. It may take you some time to get to your destination, but it will be worth it for the child and fun for you. As the child learns to move his or her body, they are also developing cognitive abilities.

You can further encourage your child's movement by handing them toys or objects that allow their hands to touch, grasp, insert, or turn. They will also try to hold items with a pincer grip—and then let go of it. Encourage them to walk, run, jump, and balance.

Order

Between the ages of one year and three and a half years old, the child will have a strong desire and need for consistency and order. It's a profound psychological need. Actually, this need for order may even be apparent within the first month of birth. The child wants repetition and routines. You may notice that at this time your child is looking to categorize their experiences. It will be challenging for them to do this if their environment is chaotic. Please do not mistake an adult's need for tidiness with your child's desire for order. The child's desire for order should be reflected in the environment. For instance, a baby will seek consistency and familiarity around them so that they can start to be grounded, oriented to their surroundings, and create a picture of the world. Any disruption or changes to their routine—even things like decorating a home or going on vacation—can cause the child distress. Please bear in mind that the environment should be organized and there should be places where everything can and should go. It is a good idea to make sure ground rules are put into place.

Senses

Around two years old, the child will develop a fascination with sensorial experiences. From the moment a baby is born, they receive external stimuli that start to activate the senses. First the sense of sight and sound are active and then touch and taste. By the time taste is activated, the child is able to put things in his/her mouth. Please bear in mind that if you try to discourage your child's need to explore their senses by saying "no" or restricting the child to a playpen, their ability to learn will be impacted.

Try to find ways your child can explore the environment using their senses. What activities can you introduce to them that are hands-on? What can you have them watch (other than TV), listen to, touch, and taste that make a fun activity?

Expressive Language

It's incredible to witness a child move from babbling as a baby, to using words as an infant, and then on to phrases, sentences, and full-blown sentences with a wider vocabulary and understanding on the child's part. From the moment your child is born, they are exposed to language. They hear the people around them talk, and if you live in a busy or lively household, they will be exposed to plenty of talk. The sensitive period for expressive language starts when children are born (and it could begin before that, too), as they hear our voices and watch us speak. They carefully observe and can feel the sensations of our speech when we hold them and talk, hum, or sing. Within just a few years of life, a child has taken in a vast quantity in relation to language.

If a child hasn't received adequate exposure to language, that lack will significantly impact their ability to communicate, and intellectual growth will be hindered. Dr. Montessori strongly believed that adults should talk to children during this sensitive period because it helps to provide children with a rich vocabulary.

To set up an environment for your child to develop language skills, you could try the following:

1. Speak to your baby or infant slowly and clearly (no baby talk after six or seven months of age).
2. Read to your child and try to change your tone of voice throughout the book, depending on what's happening in the story.

92

3. Have your infant or toddler trace letters or even try to draw letters with their fingers. Then have them match the sound of the letter with the shape. This is fun to do with sand, powder, or glitter.
4. Think of creative ways for your child to learn the alphabet. You could sing it to them.
5. Encourage your child to write, even if it's just a sentence or a few.

Music

Around the age of two or three years old, children start to become interested in rhythm, melody, pitch, and much more. They begin to develop their brains with music, and this helps to build their social, emotional, mental, and academic skills. Music will also help your child to build musical skills, of course. To give children the chance to develop strong music skills, let them have as much opportunity as possible to practice music.

We will dive deeper into music in the next chapter.

Overcoming the Desire To Correct a Child's Behavior

Some parents may not agree with the idea of not correcting children's behavior. However, with the Montessori approach, it's about having a balance between allowing them to have their freedom and guiding them to be more disciplined. Rather than telling children what to do, as a parent, you can instead help them learn inner discipline, so they will actually begin telling themselves what to do. Below are some tips to help steer the child's behavior in a way that is appropriate. This is a learning curve for you, as well as the child, because it will enable you to overcome your desire or feeling of need to correct behavior. The goal is to guide the child into realizing the natural consequences of effects brought about by their choices and actions.

It will require patience on your part as you will likely have to repeat what you are teaching, but your persistence will pay off.

1. Use clear language to emphasize a potential risk in your environment. The goal is to do it in a casual way, which can seem like a fine balance between art and science to get this right. When you set clear expectations about how your child should conduct themselves, your child will start to understand and even see the patterns of their behavior. An example of supporting a child would be saying to them: "If you want to carry that glass of orange juice to your dinner table then you should hold it like this..." or "If you want to play on the swings in the park on the way home, then just put the puzzle away and put your coat and boots on."

2. Try and help the child to think naturally about the consequences of choices. If your child wanted to do something but you know it would be detrimental, instead of saying "no" defensively, you could ask the child how they would feel if they did do what they were demanding. Ask the questions, but also mention some of the options that would present themselves should the child carry out the request. For instance, "Do you really think you would want to have chocolate ice cream for your dinner? Do you think you might end up with a sore tummy? Do you think having a nice, cooked meal will do a better job of filling you up and nourishing you?"

   By reframing how you respond to a child's request and directing them to make healthier choices, their behavior should start to adjust.

3. Allow the child to have freedom but within a range of choices. When or if your child is old enough, they may be looking to start making choices. Sometimes they will make a choice that leaves them feeling frustrated, disappointed, or upset in some way. At other times, they may not know how to make a choice, either because they have too many options to choose from or because the choice to make is a little too complicated for them to understand, and the results may not be apparent until much further down the line.

To help make it easier for your child, try to make the situation less complicated. This also includes the choices that are available to them. When you make the situation less complicated for the child, it helps them to feel like they are more in control of a situation, and as they get older, they will trust their decision-making. They will also be able to evaluate their choices better. These are skills that many adults struggle with.

If your child is really struggling or just cannot make a choice on something, then it's best to avoid giving them the choice. An empowering solution for the child could be to let them know the consequences of what will happen, and if the child does get upset, just comfort them. Try as best as possible to guide the child into focusing on the choice/s they can make. Eventually, your child will feel like they can make more complicated choices when they are ready.

The key here is to make the child's choice as simple as possible—remember the KISS method. Here is an example:

You to the child: "Would you like to wear this pair of socks or this one?"

4. Acknowledge the child's feelings and emotions. There will often be times when the child will be confused because they won't understand why they are able to make choices with some things and not others. It may leave them feeling upset or angry. If this is the case, you could acknowledge how they are feeling and allow them to experience it before trying to reason or discuss it with them. For instance, if they want to wear certain footwear but it wasn't appropriate for them to do so, they may feel upset that they couldn't make that choice. You could simply say, "You really wanted to wear your shoes today. You're not in the mood for rubber boots."

Rather than arguing with the child, who will only become more upset when you argue, by staying calm and respecting their reaction, you will help them to develop inner discipline.

CHAPTER 9:

ART AND MUSIC

One of the most important gifts you can offer your child in the Montessori home is art and music. Regularly exposing children to these will do wonders for their brain development.

Research shows that when a child learns music, it increases their ability to learn other subjects and enhances the skills they use in other areas.

When children are taught to create music, they are not just learning how to move their fingers or use their voices; they are also tapping into a variety of other skills all at the same time. For instance, they are required to use their eyes, ears, gross motor, and fine motor skills. Performing music assists in language development, increases IQ and emotional intelligence, and helps to develop spatial-temporal skills (helping them to visualize things that belong together).

Art also has significant benefits for children because it improves their creativity, confidence, and problem-solving skills, helps them to be more patient and determined. They learn the importance of holding themselves accountable for their actions and choices. If your child is creating artwork in a group, they will learn teamwork skills, the ability to be dedicated to a task or project, and how to receive constructive feedback.

Here are some reasons why children should be introduced to music and art in the early years:

1. They enhance their brain power by stimulating certain regions of the brain that are connected to academic achievement.
2. They can improve their memory.
3. They improve their social skills. Music groups and ensembles teach children how to socialize, be part of a team, develop discipline, and develop leadership skills.
4. Art and music improve language and reading skills. Toddlers learn words for colors and shapes when they create artwork.
5. They enhance critical thinking skills because children visualize when they are creating a piece of artwork. It also helps with visual-spatial skills.
6. They develop a sense of cultural awareness.

Art

When children have the option to learn art, they can develop their self-expression. It allows them the ability to communicate in ways they may not otherwise do. In a traditional school setting, arts and crafts are considered a luxury but not essential to the curriculum. More emphasis is placed on subjects that are considered relevant, such as mathematics, science, and English. This bias is quite ironic if you consider that when a young child carries out art activities, those activities actually help to boost their math skills because the skills needed to succeed in both realms are similar. For instance, they both require the ability to recognize shapes and patterns. Mathematicians and artists use geometry in their work; this includes shapes, proportion, symmetry, and measurement. There are some educators who understand the importance of children learning art. What used to be called STEM, which stands for Science, Technology, English, and Math, has now become STEAM. The A stands for Art.

There are many children who still consider themselves to be either "artistic" or a "math person." This may be due to societal conditioning from an early age. Many parents can discourage their children from pursuing a career in the arts or may criticize their abilities in a bid to dissuade them from becoming a "starving artist." While these parents have the best intentions for their child, the question we must ask is, "Why can't children be allowed to be good at both?"

When we change our mindset and help kids to understand that art and math overlap, we are providing them the opportunity to strengthen their logic and creativity. With the Montessori Method, we don't discriminate!

Fine Motor Skills and Hand-Eye Coordination Development

When children engage in artistic activities, they develop their motor skills through the movements involved in creating art, including holding a paintbrush, cutting, scribbling a line, coloring with a crayon, or playing with clay. Ideally, it's a good idea to have your child create art as early as possible. A three-year-old child can start to draw circles and will likely be ready to use safety scissors. By the time children are four years old, they will be drawing squares and will have developed their fine motor skills to be able to cut neatly or at least cut in straight lines. When children learn to cut with scissors, they are also developing manual dexterity, which they need for writing.

Hand-eye coordination is the ability to visualize or process information that you see and use it to direct and control how your hands move. We see this skill used all the time with painters, illustrators, and athletes (especially in tennis, baseball, hockey, and basketball). However, not just art and sport give us the chance to use hand-eye coordination, but also our daily lives. We tend to take our daily activities for granted, but they also afford us the opportunity to engage with hand-eye coordination.

Hand-eye coordination involves the brain, eyes, and limbs working together, and is therefore a complex process. Activities that develop this process should be encouraged in the child as early as possible. Hand-eye coordination works with fine motor skills as well as gross motor skills. If a child doesn't develop hand-eye coordination properly, they will find it difficult to perform daily tasks, which can include putting on socks, pouring a drink, and writing one's name.

The coordinated movement of the hands and eyes should naturally grow as your baby grows. While a newborn child's movement is reflexive, jerky, and often random, it will eventually become intentional, smooth, and purposeful as they continue to grow.

Finger Painting: Using Fingers As Brush

Here is an idea for your infant or toddler so that they can experience sensory exploration.

Encourage them to finger paint, using their fingers instead of a brush. You may dread the idea of having to set everything up and clean it up, but activities like this are essential for your baby's brain development.

Finger painting doesn't have to be as messy and inconvenient as you may think. Perhaps you could try the following:

1. Allow your child to paint straight onto a surface that can easily be wiped clean. If you use paper, the child will probably put it in his mouth, throw it, or flap the paper when it has paint on it!

   Here's a tip, if you would like to save your child's painting, then once the painting has been completed, simply get a piece of paper, place it on top of the painting, and rub it down until the masterpiece transfers onto the sheet of paper.

2. Could you let your child paint their masterpiece in a tub? Place your child in a tub with just a diaper on and let him have fun with the paint. When he has finished, you can rinse out the tub and proceed to wash your child.

3. It would be a wise idea for you to have wet wipes, a wet cloth, or damp paper towels handy.

4. Could you find any surfaces for your child to paint on? Silicone trays? Toy box lids? Baking sheets?

5. Try Crayola Washable Finger Paint.

6. A popular finger paint activity is "finger paint in a Ziploc." This involves putting blobs of different colored paint all over a sheet of paper or card and then insert it into a Ziploc bag and fasten

it up, sealing the paint inside the bag. Next, allow your baby or infant to play around with it. You may need to put his fingers down on the blobs of paint. The child will create art, but there won't be any mess since the paint is safe and secure in the Ziploc bag. If you would like to stick the masterpiece on the fridge, simply cut round the edges of the bag and then peel it off the painting. Allow the artwork to dry before sticking it up around the home.

Foster the Child's Imagination

Thinking independently further stimulates a child's imagination, which also allows them to produce creative work. For a Montessori parent who is looking to encourage independent thinking in your child, it would be a good idea to ask your child questions about the artwork they have created rather than make assumptions or tell them what they have created. It can be tempting for parents to make judgments or declarations, but resist the urge to do this and instead allow the child to answer your questions. An example could be, "Wow, did you paint this?" or "Wow, what did you paint?"

Music

Singing Songs for Specific Activities

There are so many ways you can have fun with encouraging your child to be musical. Playing music or singing a song doesn't have to be something you do at a specific time and then go back to "ordinary life." Singing songs can be interspersed or combined with other activities. Actually, it will be beneficial to do this because it will help to make other activities more fun, especially if it's something that your child may be quite reluctant to do. Here are some examples:

- Cleaning up
- Preparing dinner

- Sitting down
- Having a bath
- Going to the toilet/potty
- Reading books
- Getting ready for bed
- Gardening
- Dancing
- Bedtime/nap time
- Taking a walk in nature
- Traveling
- What else would your child love to do while singing songs?

Music Time

To further develop your child's listening skills and to engage them in music, why not play music (a CD or from a device, or play a musical instrument)? Choose from a variety of songs and observe how your child reacts. If they seem interested, stop and listen, making sure to point to your ears and talk about the word "listen."

Make a Music Shelf

You may decide to make a music shelf using instruments that you know your child will love to explore independently. If you're not sure what instruments your child would be interested in, start off by introducing them to one or two different types of instruments and see how they respond.

To really get your child excited, you could create a theme for your child's music shelf. For instance, what do they love? Does he love gardening? Perhaps you could have a botany-themed music shelf. Does she love dogs? Perhaps you could decorate the shelf with things relating to dogs. Or even a musician. There are many ideas. You could even change the theme, depending on what events are taking place throughout the year. Instruments you could consider include:

- Assorted wooden instruments
- Xylophone
- The Montessori bells, which will help your child to develop musical hearing
- Rainstick (you can always make them yourself if you'd prefer)
- Homemade: beans in a plastic soda bottle rattle for your baby to shake

Please note, if you are going to make your own instruments, please make sure they are safe. For instance, if you do make the beans in a plastic bottle rattle instrument, you must make 100% sure that the cap is glued on securely.

Inclusion of Music and Movement

Dr. Montessori knew the importance for children to experience a combination of music and movement in their environment. Today, scientists have come to this understanding as well. Neurologists now realize that music and movement together help to give children a sense of belonging, a chance for self-expression, and an opportunity to develop their coordination skills. Movement also enhances learning and, most importantly for the child, it's fun! Children love to move and should do so. Encouraging them to dance along to the music will also lift their spirits. Ideally, you want to encourage them to dance or move their bodies in some way, as often as possible. Perhaps your child could dance to her bedroom when it's time to get ready for bed. Or he could do a little "bedtime jiggle."

You don't have to be a musician, singer, or dancer to have your child become stimulated and musically intuitive. It's simple. Allow them to have fun and you do the same. They can just shake their body however they want to at that moment. Encourage them to try different dance styles, too, to see which one/s they like.

Here are some ways you can include music and movement:

- Provide instruments such as egg shakers, bells and maracas.

- Make associations between songs and their activities, such as brushing teeth, helping to prepare dinner, etc.
- Sing when it's time to transition your child into another activity, such as getting ready for bed or preparing the meal.

Home Activities

For the Newborn

- Make shakers by putting beans, rice, metal bolts, pebbles, or sand into a bottle (once again, make sure they are completely safe).
- You could put out a few different types of instruments and see which ones they like to play with.
- Sing to them.
- Finger paint.
- Show images that are colorful or have a variety of shapes.
- Have music on in the background for them to listen to.
- Let them see you dance and hear you sing.
- Encourage other family members to dance and sing around your child.
- Play classical or relaxation music in the background.
- Play different types of music and watch their reaction. Then you will know what kind of music interests them at this stage.

For the Infant

- Allow them the opportunity to hear different songs.
- Play musical chairs.
- Ask them to paint or draw a song.
- Encourage them to experiment with color.
- Find music that will encourage your child to march, skip,

gallop, etc. as the mood of the song or the tempo changes.

- Sing songs that involve clapping and dancing.
- Invite friends and family to join you and play their instruments, sing, or dance if they have skills in these areas.
- Take your child to visit a museum so they can look at the art pieces.
- Read books on artists and musicians to them or with them.
- Encourage them to help make costumes or other arts and craft projects with you for special occasions such as Christmas, birthdays, Easter, etc.
- Encourage them to become familiar with musical notes through sound and sight.
- If you happen to have several musical instruments in your home, get the child to close their eyes as someone plays each one. Have the child guess the instrument being played.

For the Toddler

- Drawing
- Cutting
- Painting
- Read books about the lives of musicians.
- Play a musical instrument and ask them to guess what it is.
- Dance with them at random times of the day and encourage them to do the same with you.
- Encourage them to do self-portraits by having a mirror in front of them.
- Sewing
- Arts and crafts
- Clay pottery
- Have them perform at a "make-believe" drum parade.
- Have them learn a musical instrument.
- Have music playing in the background as you have your child

carry out a "walking on the line" activity.

- Encourage them to draw or paint their favorite characters in a book.
- Encourage them to sit in nature and draw what they see or feel inspired to draw.

If you are uncomfortable or shy about singing, then you can do a couple of things:

1. Break out of your comfort zone and do it anyway.
2. Listen to popular children's songs and sing along until you start to feel comfortable, and then you can sing to them (or play an instrumental version) of the songs.

CHAPTER 10:

MAKING MONTESSORI AT HOME WORK FOR YOU

Many parents feel overwhelmed when it comes to creating a Montessori home environment. There is a lot to take in. However, as we mentioned earlier in the guide, you are learning along with your child, and it isn't necessary to incorporate everything all at once. It's better not to do that because both you and your child may feel overwhelmed. If you have a newborn child, it will be easier to start introducing Montessori right away than if your child is a little older. Nevertheless, no matter the age of your child, they will greatly benefit and adjust quickly.

One of the many wonderful things about Montessori is that it can be applied to most settings. Many parents or caregivers get worried that if they don't have an entire playroom, they won't be able to apply the methods. Even if you have a small space, you can still create Montessori at home because it's about making the most of what you have, not what you don't have. This is a perfect opportunity to get really creative. Here are four ways you can implement Montessori at home regardless of how much space you have:

1. Less is more! When you look at other Montessori home environments on blog posts, social media, etc., you will notice that there aren't a lot of materials and the items they have are few, high quality, creative, and colorful or stimulating. This is

the Montessori way! Any activities that are on display should be the ones your child is currently working with. They should be age-appropriate. Remember, the younger your child is, the fewer items or toys they will need. You will need to provide some more resources once your child grows, and their skills and abilities develop—but it doesn't have to be a lot more.

Since children are looking for order at this stage, it's much better for them if there is no clutter and very little materials around. That way, things are organized, and it's clear to them where things are so that they have easier access to what they want or need. This is how they will develop independence. A chaotic environment will likely result in a chaotic child!

If you have a small shelf in a room that's just for your child, then that's fine. If you have no space to dedicate a whole room to a Montessori environment, then that's absolutely fine too. Again, use what space you can. As long as your child can see the space and it's presented with careful consideration and organization, that's what is important. Work with the spaces you have, find ways to clear out what really isn't being used, and transform it into beautiful Montessori space.

2. If things don't look aesthetically pleasing to you, it's likely that they won't to your child either. Just remember to present materials in a way that looks appealing and will interest your child. It's a good idea to make sure that your child has their own space, but it should be a part of the family setting and not completely separate. When they go off to play, they shouldn't be cut off from the rest of the family.

3. Use pretty, naturally woven baskets to help you organize materials and activities. A basket or even something else that's made from wood or natural materials will help you to store the child's activities neatly, especially if they are being kept in the common area of the home along with other household items. You can easily find these at a thrift store. Your storage boxes,

baskets, or trays don't have to match either. It may be pleasing to your child's eye to have them not match!

4. Focus on practical life activities.

Suiting Materials & Activities To Meet Needs

Many parents get overwhelmed with the feeling they need to have both the right amount of space and the right materials. Many people believe that if they don't have all the equipment, materials, and resources, they won't be able to apply the Montessori Methods properly. That's not the case. The purpose of Montessori at home is to involve the child in everyday activities and encourage them to feel like a valuable family member who is contributing to the home. A simple way to do this is to get them involved in practical life activities. For instance, if you have a small water bottle and a cloth, you can have your child help you wash the windows. You can even sing songs at the same time. If you are folding freshly washed laundry, why not have your child see if they can match up the socks for you? It can be as simple as that.

It's important not to force your child to do practical life activities. For instance, it's not necessary to tell your child they have to stop whatever activity they are doing to help you with the dishes. Instead, if you naturally make the practical life activities fun and exercise patience as they are learning, eventually they will want to help. Remember, children have a desire to be useful, and helping out gives them a sense of achievement. Many activities can be started before the child can even walk. For instance, they can sit down and sort laundry by color. Every child's learning needs are different. If you have more than one child, you will likely understand this as well. You know your child well and will be able to determine if an activity or certain materials are suitable for your child.

In the beginning, you may or may not have an idea of what materials and activities your child wants or needs. However, this is where your "scientific research" will come in handy. You will quickly develop an understanding of what they require, the more you observe them. Then it will be easier to provide some of those materials.

Changing & Adapting

You will find that as your child grows, their needs, desires, preferences, and behaviors will change. This means you will be changing too. What works amazingly well in your Montessori home when the child is a newborn will need to be adjusted by the time your child grows to an infant and toddler. It's important that you anticipate change and are open to it. Otherwise, it will hinder your child's ability to progress in daily life and develop as a person. Since children at this early age are looking for routine and order, there is bound to be discomfort for a short period when changes are made around the home. It's best to make any changes that are needed as gently as possible, taking into account how it will impact your child. Children can become very attached to certain items such as toys. However, if you can see that the toy is starting to look a little worse for wear, or is broken and cannot be fixed, then it needs to go into the trash. Of course, the child may become upset. Just be as understanding as possible rather than getting upset with them for crying or having a tantrum. You could also use this experience to help your child learn about releasing things and emotions.

You may find that your child suddenly gets bored with an activity or hates it in the first place. That's fine. Don't try to force them to do this activity if they don't like it. This goes against the Montessori approach. They may let you know verbally or nonverbally what their interests are. Remember, we want to guide children with their choices of activity. Any activities or equipment that are no longer in use can be taken out of the home. It's important to do this; otherwise you risk your home becoming cluttered.

The Need for Continued Learning

You are going to find that unexpected things will come up in daily life, and you may not be sure of the best course of action. This is natural and happens with all parents. As a conscious Montessori parent, you may question your actions and choices at times, and that's fine. Please know it's important that you give yourself permission to keep studying the Montessori approach because there's a lot of information to absorb. The further resources section at the back of this guide provides links to blogs, videos, and social media accounts to help further educate you. Here are some ways you can further educate yourself.

Popular Blogs

There are many popular blogs out there that are dedicated to the topic of Montessori at home. Many of these blogs are run by parents like you, who are dedicated to raising the best human beings possible with the resources that are available to them. Many parents have made what they may call "mistakes" along the way, and they share their experiences on their blogs. You will find blogs that relate to specific concepts of the Montessori Method as well as those that discuss all of the areas.

Over time, you may even decide to set up a blog yourself so that you can share your experiences with other parents and caregivers to further help you on this journey.

Ideas and Inspiration on Instagram and Pinterest

If you ever need some inspiration on how to create your environment, then Instagram and Pinterest are ideal places to visit. Many Montessori parents like to post images or create pinboards that show how their home environment is set up when the child is a newborn, infant, and toddler. As you browse through the countless photos, you'll notice that many differ from each other, which should reassure you that there is no right or wrong way to create your own Montessori environment.

There are a lot of ideas for DIY projects and activities, so if you're concerned about your budget or space, don't be! Start a pinboard on Pinterest and save your favorite pins on Montessori ideas so you can easily refer to them. You will never be short on ideas and inspiration. If anything, this is what can overwhelm parents. However, I would like to remind you again that it's a good idea to keep it simple. If you find yourself spending hours at a time looking through Instagram posts or Pinterest boards, it may be time to look away so that you don't feel stuck. There are many beautiful home environments that others have created, and seeing them can leave you feeling doubtful of what you can create. The key is not to allow yourself to get too caught up in other people's ideas that you don't believe in your own. Also, it can be very easy for many new Montessori parents to feel inadequate or disheartened because they compare themselves to what other parents are doing. The purpose of using social media is to uplift you and open you up to a wide range of possibilities for your child. It should inspire. If you find yourself feeling discouraged, then step away for a while. You will also find articles, videos, and blog posts on how to deal with feeling overwhelmed or uncertain when it comes to setting up a Montessori environment at home.

The Power of Connecting With Other Caregivers

The Montessori way of parenting requires a great deal of thought and attention because you are encouraging your child to be independent, creative, confident, and self-sufficient. This is an entirely different approach to a parent who does everything for their child. You may sometimes find it difficult to relate to parents who do use the traditional parenting style, expecting their child to rely on them for everything for many years. You may also find that they find it quite difficult to relate to your Montessori parenting style.

If you're feeling stuck or anxious at any point, don't suffer in silence. You really aren't alone because the Montessori at home approach is proving to be more popular. Make sure you reach out to someone who is on a similar journey to you. Many caregivers are happy to help and are always looking to connect with like-minded people. Remind yourself that you don't have to go through this journey alone. So, reach out to other caregivers who share your interest and belief in raising children in a

Montessori environment. You will find a wealth of online communities and also see if there are offline groups you can attend. You may decide to join both online and offline groups, and that's completely fine. If you join a community and find you don't resonate with it, simply try another one. You are not limited in your connections.

When you become part of a community, it will help you to deepen your understanding and learning because you can share ideas, frustrations, and solutions. Other caregivers may have a different take on how to implement something, and it could be useful for you to be open to their point of view. If you ever have a problem you aren't sure how to tackle, you will likely come across a caregiver who has had similar experiences and can advise you or give you tips and suggestions.

It's important that you do not allow other people's opinions to drown out your own, even if you are new to setting up Montessori at home, and they've been doing it for many years. While someone else's opinion and advice can be very useful, it is you who is the real expert on what is right for you to implement in your home and the needs of your child. Still, you will learn a lot from joining groups and it will make it more fun for you. Over time you may decide to meet up with your new online friends for playdates.

CONCLUSION

By now, you should have gained a good understanding of the Montessori approach and how it can be implemented in the home. Unlike the traditional classroom and parenting style, where the adult tells the child what to learn, do, be, and when, the Montessori approach is a groundbreaking way that encourages independence from an early age. The adult doesn't dictate to the child about what they need to know, nor do they punish the child for not learning or for not being interested in what is taught. The traditional style of learning is quite conflicting. For instance, children are expected to start talking, walking, and moving about by the time they are toddlers, and yet when they start to do those things, they are reprimanded for it. They are told to "be quiet" and "keep still."

Very few people question this way of bringing up children. However, over the century, there have been some people who have questioned it and then gone on to create something innovative. Dr. Maria Montessori is one of those people. She created the Montessori Method, which has become increasingly popular in recent years thanks to well known public figures like Amazon founder Jeff Bezos and Google founder Larry Page, both of whom received Montessori educations. There are many other people who are in the public eye and have gone on to achieve great things, and they have also been public about how Montessori school greatly helped them.

The Montessori Method educates children to be self-directive by allowing them to participate in hands-on activities that are fun, stimulating, and collaborative. The activities a child undertakes are designed to engage their five senses of touch, taste, smell, sound, and sight. Dr. Montessori found that when these senses are stimulated through activities, it increases a child's intellectual development. She carried out a large amount of research on how children learn and behave. She found that up to the age of six, a child is very susceptible to their environment. This is an important time because whatever they learn at this point will impact how they show up in the world as adults. If they are nurtured, encouraged, supported, and raised in a safe environment, they are highly likely to grow up as confident, balanced adults. The Montessori Method will help a child to:

1. Become independent from an early age
2. Receive an education that is focused on child-centered learning
3. Be creative and imaginative
4. Develop self-control and self-discipline
5. Develop a high level of emotional and intellectual intelligence
6. Become socially confident

As your child gets older, you are sure to discover more benefits. However, you may even notice them in your newborn!

Adults often forget that children are intelligent beings and so they address them as if they know very little and need talking down to. However, by choosing to read this guide, you have started your journey on a different and amazing path. Your role as a Montessori parent is to be a guide to your child as they decide what they would like to learn. Their preferences for activities will change as they get older, and you will need to alter the Montessori home to reflect this. Children have a natural tendency to want to learn, and they also have a desire to contribute to their household or the community at large. They just need to be encouraged to do these things. If you introduce them to practical life skills from an early age (the earlier, the better), they will want to contribute towards activities that are considered "boring" or "chores" to the non-Montessori child.

In this guide, you have learned about the guiding principles of the

Montessori Method, which include:

- The child is free to explore his/her environment.
- The child is a master of his/her own learning.
- The child learns through his/her senses.
- The child needs a safe and nurturing environment.

At the start of this guide you may have had a lot of questions about how you, as a parent, could start to incorporate the Montessori principles into your child's life. The intention of this guide is to leave you feeling more confident as you embark on your journey as a Montessori parent.

You now have the knowledge and the resources at your fingertips to be an empowering Montessori parent.

One of the biggest takeaways from this book is that the child should be free to explore their environment, and it's imperative you ensure the environment is safe for them to do so. For instance, your room/s should be childproof. If it means getting down on your hands and knees so that you can perceive things from your child's height, then please do so.

Another major message of this book is that you don't need to feel overwhelmed or stressed out about creating a Montessori home. Many parents are worried that because they have limited space or a tight budget, they aren't going to be able to design an ideal Montessori home or that they won't be able to get it "right."

There is no such thing as the "right" Montessori home because what will work for one parent and their child won't work for someone else. Also, you can create a stunning Montessori home without having a lot of space. There are a lot of parents who have created videos, blog posts, Instagram images and Pinterest boards where they have highlighted how they have made good use of confined space. Even if it's having a shelf in the corner of the living room, what matters is that your child finds it interesting.

It would be great for you to reach out and connect with other parents who believe in the Montessori movement. This will deepen your understanding of Montessori because you will be able to share insights, ask questions, and meet up for playdates.

The first six years of a child's life have them dipping in and out of sensitive periods. Sensitive periods are when children are even more impressionable with their environment. They take everything in like a sponge, so patience and consistency are needed at these times. But those investments will be worth it. You now have ideas for various activities that your child can do to develop through each sensitive period, which include small objects, movement, order, senses, expressive language, and music. Each of these is very important and has significant benefits for the child.

If you are creative or on a budget, you can always make furniture, toys, etc. to suit your child's needs. Many of the blogs on Montessori parenting give tips and advice on how to make your own resources and materials. I hoped to leave you with practical steps you can take to set up your Montessori home, and now you can go and start implementing what you have learned. Please do not feel like you have to integrate *everything*. It would not be practical or beneficial for you or your child. Your child should ideally have an environment that is clutter-free, organized, stimulating, and calm. They strongly desire order at this stage in their development because they are looking to understand the world and discover their identities. If your home is chaotic, it will be stressful for them. If you offer them too many activities at any given time, they will feel overwhelmed and will not be able to focus properly.

Your child will thrive with a few high-quality toys and activities that can always be rotated. The Montessori equipment and materials were designed for a reason—they support the Montessori approach. The floor bed, weaning table and chair, child-size utensils and furniture, etc. all allow the child to become independent and be more in control of their daily lives with you as their guide. However, you can substitute, so please don't worry about the cost of all this or where you will fit them in your home.

This is all much information to digest, and it would be a good idea for you to re-read this book, as well as look into other resources that are listed in the further resources section. Most of all, please take a moment to congratulate yourself for the effort you are putting into being the best parent to your child. Your choice today to bring Montessori into the home is going to serve your child well as he/she continues to journey through life, and while he/she develops into an independent, strong thinker. Your child will ultimately have you to thank for setting him/her off on that journey.

The best of luck to you.

I'D LOVE YOUR HELP

As a self-publishing author, reviews are the lifeblood of my work.
I would be over-the-moon thankful if you could take just 60 seconds to leave a brief review on Amazon.
I know you must be busy and I truly appreciate your time, even a few short sentences would be greatly helpful.

Don't forget to get your complimentary

7 FREE MONTESSORI GAMES FOR THE HOME

(DIY Games for the Kids That Are Worth Your Time!)

I hope you've enjoyed reading this book about applying the Montessori educational system at home. Here are a few ideas to help you bring Montessori into your home quickly.

What you'll get:

- 7 free games you can play at home;
- How to use home tools to create the games;
- Specific instructions on how to use the final products with your kids.

The Montessori educational system is ideal for all children!
Follow the link down below to download the games:

http://gracestockholm.net/montessori-education-at-home/

BONUS SECTION:
GUIDED MEDITATION FOR PARENTS AND KIDS

In this bonus section, I have prepared 2 special guided meditation sessions, 45 minutes each.

The first is for you, the parent. Meditating is a great way to relieve stress and keep composure throughout our hectic lives. In this meditation, we will focus on the connection with our inner child which will enable you to better understand and cope with your child, even in challenging times and situations.

The second session is for your child. In this session your child will learn the benefits of meditating as well as be more empowered and focused. You will probably want to sit with your child for this session, at least for the first few times. If you have a younger child and the session is too long for them, simply do a few minutes at a time and gradually increase the meditation time.

If this is the audio version, just dive in.

If this is the kindle or paperback version, sit down and read it to yourself slowly.

Session #1 - For You

-Welcome to this meditation session for parents. In the following minutes, you and I will embark on a quest to find the qualities of the outstanding parent you wish to be. You know you are a great parent, but a great parent is not just a caretaker for his or her child. He or she is also an observer.

-One of the most important aspects of being a parent is being able to not just direct, but observe and let your child be free while providing a safe environment for them. Have them play their favorite games and allow them to learn from them on their own.

-What I want you to do before all else is to simply relax. Find a place where you feel at ease with yourself and the surroundings - it can be in your house, in a garden or even in the car.

-Once you find that spot, I want you to sit comfortably. If you choose a chair, ideally choose one that has a back. Fix your back in the chair and have your arms sitting comfortably on your lap. Your neck should be erect and your head held upright comfortably, not tense in any way.

-Once you've found this position, it is time to begin this meditation practice. First, I want you to notice the simple act of your breathing. All you have to do is mentally notice how your body breaths.

-Remember that we are still early in this practice, so you don't have to change anything about your posture, your breathing or anything else. Just let the mind do what it does best, think about whatever it wants while you gently observe the breathing as if it was your child.

-And as you do so, start noticing how the chest expands while you inhale the air into the lungs, as well as how it contracts while the air is pushed out of the body. Simply sit with this feeling for a few moments, eyes open and relaxed, while simply experiencing life as it is right now.

-Awesome! Now, we will focus on the next part of the practice, which means I will ask you to take a couple of big, deep breaths right now. As the body breathes it creates a unique, lively sensation, as the air moves in and out of it. Breath in through the nose, and then out through the mouth. Do it gently, but loud enough so that you can hear the breathing easily.

-Breath like this for the next 15 seconds or so.

-And with this final exhale through the mouth, gently close your eyes and let your breath come back to its natural rhythm. This can be in and out through the nose, in through the nose and out through the mouth or in and out through the mouth. Regardless of how you feel like breathing, it's important to keep breathing like your body dictates, naturally, until the end of the practice.

-With the breath now back to its normal state, we're going to be focusing on the act of letting the body be the way it wants to be. Just like you would a child who's learning new things, being curious about anything and everything around them.

-We will begin with a scanning of the body. The only thing you have to do is to observe and learn from how the body feels. You will not mingle with your feelings and emotions. You will simply observe them as they come and go and then move to the next part of the body.

-Start the observation at the bottom of the legs. See how your toes are feeling right now, as well as your feet and bottom part of the legs.

-Observe the way the legs are feeling right now. See if they're relaxed and calm, or if they're tense or stressed for any reason. Remember to just observe, not try and change anything about it. And while focusing on the different parts of the body, remember to just keep a gentle focus on the breath.

-Move to the knees and the upper part of your legs right now. Observe the way the knees, so important to the movement of your body, feel right at this moment. Regardless if they're tense or relaxed, simply notice the feeling and then move on to the upper part of the legs.

-You are now going to move to the middle part of the body. Gently scan this area of the body up to the base of the stomach, noticing the way it feels.

-Once you've noticed how the middle of the body feels, the center of gravity, move up to the stomach area and the lower back. Observe the way the stomach is right now. Don't be judgmental. Simply notice if there's any discomfort or if the stomach is nice and at ease, and do the same with the lower back.

-Very well! It is now time to move up to the chest area, the heart and the upper back. The place where the entire body gets fueled with blood and oxygen. Start by noticing if there's any tension in the heart at all. If it beats regularly or if it goes a tad slower, or faster than normal. Simply observe and learn from it, like you would observe your child learning new things in life through play. The heart is your child and one of your most important assets. Taking good care of it is at the base of a good life.

-You are now going to move your attention to the neck and face. Observe these two parts of your body closely. Is there any grimace on your face you weren't aware about a moment ago? If that's the case, just observe it and let the natural rhythm of the breath take care of it. If the neck is too tight, focus on your breathing and feel how it aligns with the body.

-You are doing very well. Before moving to the top of the body, take a few moments to focus on the breath passing through it. Starting from the nose and mouth and going down the neck and all the way to the lungs. Filling the lungs and then releasing the air on the exhale. Good, you are doing wonderfully.

-Finally, move your point of focus to the top of your head. Stay with whatever feeling you encounter while scanning this topmost part of your entire body. This is the space where all of your thoughts, emotions and feelings are being created every single moment of your life. Take a few moments to appreciate the beauty of this machine that works calmly and always for you.

-And as you are getting done with experiencing the last few moments in silence with your head, simply observing the way it is right now, we're going to move to a short visualization game.

-For a brief moment now, I want you to imagine yourself as a small child. I do not mean for you to remember how you were in the past when you were little. I want you to imagine yourself in a room filled with toys and books and everything that is fun to a child.

-You can be dressed how you want, you can sit on the floor or in a chair, you can do whatever it is that you want to do.

-What I want you to do now is to simply observe the child as silently as possible. Observe the way he or she learns from playing with the toys and books in the room. Observe the mistakes he or she makes while doing whatever activity they want. And whatever you do, whatever you see the child doing, resist the urge to judge or correct them.

-Simply let the child evolve and grow in front of your eyes while keeping a safe eye on them. That's all you need to do right now, observe the child while sitting quietly and keeping a gentle focus on your breath.

-Breath in through the nose, and then release the air from your lungs out through the mouth.

-Imagine the child stepping over a book or a small toy. They start screaming and your initial reaction is one of anger. But this time what you have to do is just observe and keep yourself silent. Let the child go through the pain and let them see how to overcome it.

-Although hard for a parent to keep themselves from comforting their child in pain, at times all you need to do is be there. You do not need to solve the problem, you do not need to offer solutions all the time, you do not need to even speak. Just be there. The child will overcome their anger or frustration and will strengthen their new personality with better skills for self-protection and awareness. They grow a more empowered version of themselves and a more focused individual, no matter how young they are.

-Let the child take care of the pain and observe how they do it. It is not a dangerous injury; therefore, you don't have to react in any way but just sit with the situation until it is naturally solved by itself. The child is already back at play and starts learning new things right now.

-Moving forward, we will focus on a new scenario. Imagine the child running to the stove and touching its hot surface. The child's first temptation is to pull their hand back, which they naturally do. After this, the child begins to cry and becomes agitated by the idea that they have been injured. They begin to cry, shout and pound around.

-As natural as it may come for you as the parent to want and help the kid now, the best thing you can do for them is to simply hug them and let them be. Let them acknowledge the pain, the heat creating the pain, the action that took them where they are now, in a painful situation. This is a simple lesson which you can let your child deal with and have them learn by example. Their example. Surely, if we could stop the child before the injury, we should do so. But in this situation in our mind, it already happened so let's try to learn from it.

-Leave the child be, let them take care of alleviating the pain, however they might want to do this. This small injury is nothing too serious so that it needs your intervention. Therefore, you can let things develop in a natural way and leave the child to cope and learn on their own. They will be back playing with their toys in no time, having learned a valuable lesson about fire and pain along the way.

-Next, what I want you to do is to imagine the child in the kitchen. There's a huge bowl of flour on the counter. The bowl is made out of glass, filled with flour to the brim. In an attempt to play around, the child picks up the bowl and drops it on the floor. The flour spills all over the kitchen, the bowl shatters into dozens of pieces and the child freezes on the spot, panicking.

-At this moment, the parent would go ahead and comfort the kid. Or, in some cases, they would start shouting and panicking the child even more. Whatever the case might be, the best approach here is to simply let things run their course, of course once there's no physical hazard to the child. Visualize yourself doing this for the small child. Allow them to be.

-Let the little one deal with the situation. Let them get their faces cleaned, let them see the situation from their perspective. Let them cry and be kids. Do not interfere with the natural processes of acknowledging and asserting the situation. This is as natural of a situation as it can be, so simply let it unfold. This way, you're teaching your child a much more valuable lesson.

-Visualizations are important to develop mental clarity and models. It makes you realize just how powerful the simple act of imagining things can be. By visualizing a possible scenario, you'll have a much better coping mechanism for when the actual events will unfold.

-Breath in through the nose now. And then out through the mouth. We'll resume our visualization right away.

-During the next few moments, we will use the intervention technique in our visualizations. Instead of simply letting the child be, we will step in to their worries and use our best judgement to make things better while still keeping our distance.

-Once again, breath in through the nose, and then slowly out through the mouth.

-I now need you to imagine the little child coming back from school and being upset. They are unwilling to share at the moment so you leave them be for a while but things don't seem to get any better. When you ask them to come down for dinner, they refuse. This is where you will naturally be inclined to go ahead and see what went wrong at school. Unlike the pain scenarios that unfolded and are over in a minute or so, this is more of a psychological unrest rather than a physical one.

-Once you're in the child's room, begin by walking up to them and asking them simple questions. "Is everything all right?" or "How was school today, all good there?" should be simple, general questions that are not so intrusive so that your child will pull back but rather open up and talk about their worries. When they start talking, your only job is to listen until they pause for an opinion, answer or advice.

-Usually, things that happen at school can be either related to mocking or bullying, a bad grade, or a bad relationship turnout for older kids. Whatever the case might be, you have to be supportive for the kid. Even if you get a sense that it's not entirely someone else's responsibility for their situation. Using phrases like "I get you, I do" or "I see where you're coming from, I understand", will ensure the kid knows they're not alone.

-In this visualization, the child is upset because a classmate has received a higher grade than they did in biology class. Imagine yourself comforting this child in such a manner, you're not only giving them encouragement but also helping them understand why they might've gotten a lower grade than somebody else.

-You start saying something like "I understand why you're upset. Low grades may not be not fun to get. But you also need to remember that your grade is not a reflection of who you are. When you compare it to your classmate's, then yes, it's lower, but that does not say anything about you. It's just another grade. You can work on your biology skills later if this bothers you. And on the next test, you will surely get a much better grade!"

-Breath in through the nose, and then out through the mouth as we are now about to leave the visualization part of this meditation behind us. You've done great!

-As we're moving closer and closer to the end of this meditation practice, I want you to focus on a new idea.

-I want you to reflect upon how important play is for a child's learning process. Even if playtime is almost always separated from traditional learning time in child growth, the two can and should be combined for a pleasurable experience for the young.

-Just like the imagined version of you enjoyed reading books and playing with the toys at the same time, learning from your mistakes and accumulating new ideas and knowledge, so you have to keep in mind the fact that learning through play is important for your own children.

-Over the next few moments of this practice today, we will be focusing on a few affirmations. An affirmation is a powerful statement that, once you hear and incorporate into your system, it gets you ready to face whatever the adversity of the situation described might be.

-During the next few minutes, we will be focusing on affirmations that are related to the Montessori way of parenting. Using learning and logical games to raise a more independent child. Letting your child learn from their own mistakes. Nurturing their needs when necessary and letting them be when they can take care of themselves.

-Here we go for the first few affirmations. Remember to keep a gentle focus on the breath as we move along.

-We will go through the affirmations slowly, twice for each one.

-Let's start with the first one: Joy, feeling one's own value, being appreciated and loved by others, feeling useful and capable of production are all factors of enormous value for the human soul. Once more: Joy, feeling one's own value, being appreciated and loved by others, feeling useful and capable of production are all factors of enormous value for the human soul.

-Very well. Get ready for the next one by breathing in and out through the nose gently.

-The child is the builder of man. Every man or woman ware once a child, and every child grows into a man or woman. Again: The child is the builder of man. Every man or woman ware once a child, and every child grows into a man or woman.

-Great! Have a quick mental pause and focus on the breath before the next affirmation.

-One of the greatest signs of success for a parent is to be able to know that their children can cope on their own with both simple and complex situations. Once again: One of the greatest signs of success for a parent is to be able to know that their children can cope on their own with both simple and complex situations.

-Awesome knowledge in this last one! Have a breath before we move along to the next one.

-To assist the child, while leaving them free, is the basic task of the ideal parent. To assist the child, while leaving them free, is the basic task of the ideal parent.

-Amazingly well done. Breath in through the nose, and then out, through the mouth. A new affirmation awaits, so become fully aware.

-Personal health is related to self-control and to the worship of life in all its natural beauty - self-control bringing with it happiness, renewed youth, and long life. Once more: Personal health is related to self-control and to the worship of life in all its natural beauty - self-control bringing with it happiness, renewed youth, and long life.

-We will now take a few moments to stay with the new affirmations in peace. Letting them all sink in before moving to the next series of states. As you do this, gently touch the base of your chest. Find the point of contact where the breathing happens in the body. When you do so, bring your entire awareness to that one point. Nothing else is important right now but that point where the breath happens. Move the hand back to where it was and keep focusing on that point of breathing while letting the entire being be enhanced by the affirmations you've just heard.

-Good. Now, we will move to the final part of the affirmations with another set of five. Here we go.

-If help and salvation are to come, they will come from the children, for the children are the makers of man. If help and salvation are to come, they will come from the children, for the children are the makers of man.

-What a great piece of wisdom here! Great, breath in through the nose, then out through the mouth. You are doing great.

-Next: it is incredible to notice that even from the earliest age, kids find the greatest satisfaction in feeling independent. The exalting feeling of being sufficient to oneself comes as a revelation.

Again: it is incredible to notice that even from the earliest age, kids find the greatest satisfaction in feeling independent. The exalting feeling of being sufficient to oneself comes as a revelation.

-Amazing. Remember to keep a gentle focus on the point of breathing in the body. Let's move on to the next one.

-Education is not something which a parent does, rather it is a natural process which develops spontaneously in the human being. Education is protection for life, education accompanies life during its whole course. And again: Education is not something which a parent does, rather it is a natural process which develops spontaneously in the human being. Education is protection for life, education accompanies life during its whole course.

-Wonderful. Have a quick mental pause again here, letting it all sink in. Breathing in through the nose, and then out through the mouth as we continue to the next affirmation.

- The ultimate gift we can provide for our children is to prepare them for what the world has instore. Again: The ultimate gift we can provide for our children is to prepare them for what the world has instore.

-Good job! We are getting closer to the end of the affirmations part of this practice now. Get ready for the last one, coming right now.

- The consciousness of knowing how to make oneself useful, how to help mankind in many ways, fills the soul with noble confidence, almost religious dignity. One more time: The consciousness of knowing how to make oneself useful, how to help mankind in many ways, fills the soul with noble confidence, almost religious dignity.

-What a great session of affirmations this one was! Congratulations for going through with it and expanding your knowledge with some ideologies of Montessori education. Remember to get back to these affirmations every time you feel overwhelmed applying this technique for your own kids. When you feel like you're about to slip simply go back to the practice and remember these affirmations for more clarity and calm.

-Now comes the time to slowly get back to everyday life, as we move along and towards the end of this meditation session.

-Before going about our day now, we will slowly regain our conscious state after the meditative one by engaging our senses into the world outside of our mind and body. Bringing the body back to the present moment doesn't mean you have to leave this meditative, calm state behind for the day. On the contrary, it means you will be left feeling at ease, relaxed and ready for whatever life brings.

-Begin by shifting your attention from the breath to any sounds you might be hearing. They can be outside sounds from people outside your house, cars passing by or planes flying somewhere in the distance. Or they can be sounds from inside the body, like the beating heart in the middle of your chest.

-Now, move to the sense of touch and feel the body as it sits in the chair or on the floor, depending on where you've sat during the practice today. Feel the sensation of touch all through the body, even if it is just air touching your face or clothing that touches your arms or legs.

-Use the sense of smell to see if you can grasp any smells inside the room you're in right now. Is there any smell that's soft, like that of a flower, or are there any smells that are strong, like a perfume or the smell of old books?

-Finally, what I want you to do to end this meditation session is to simply take a deep breath in through the nose. And as you get ready to exhale through the mouth, gently, softly open the eyes. Feel the visual spectrum filling with imagery from the room you're in. Don't judge anything that you see but just observe the many objects.

-Take a moment to appreciate the sense of calm and stillness meditation has brought in for you today. And remember to keep that sense of observation all throughout the day today.

-You have done great! Congratulations, you are now ready to implement the Montessori educational system with your own child at home. Be proud of your accomplishment and use it to enhance the great being that is your child.

-Remember to always get back to the present moment whatever it is that you'll be doing today and the days ahead. Whenever you feel you are having troubles applying the great knowledge of the Montessori education system, simply come back to this meditation practice or to the book.

-Thank you for joining me for this practice.

Session #2 - For Your Child

-Hi there, and welcome to this meditation practice specifically designed for you to have fun and explore today! We are going to take a little journey down meditation road today, which is a game designed to make you feel better and be more empowered. Ready to have some fun? Alright, here we go!

-First, I want you to leave everything that you're doing right now and just find that place in your room where you feel most comfortable. It can be your favorite chair, or it can be your bed or even somewhere on the floor, wherever is cozy and nice.

-Are you there yet? Good, now that you're all comfy and cozy, we're going to move on. Meditation, if you don't know it by now, is like a game for the human mind. It's a fun game, one that's like no other game you've ever played before.

-It requires no toys, no props, no roller coasters. Although a roller coaster sounds fun, doesn't it? All it requires from you is a little attention and a speck of dedication. And the will to have some fun by using nothing but the mind. Just like your favorite superheroes do!

-To start the meditation game, or practice, or session, you can call it whichever way you want, all you have to do is close your eyes as you take a few deep breaths. I'm not talking normal deep breaths, like you'd take after running around playing with the dog outside.

-Before you take these breaths though, what I want you to do is to just start and feel your body. Yes, you will need to sort of check how the body feels. It might sound weird but when was the last time you've taken a good look at how your body was doing? Have you ever done that? Maybe not, but that's fine. Here's your chance to do it.

-Start by noticing the points of contact that your body has right now with whatever it is that you sit on. Maybe it's the feet on the floor if you're in a chair, arms on your lap, back pressed against the chair. Maybe you're sitting on the bed, which extends the surface of contact and therefore makes it easier for you to feel the body.

-Now please take a moment to reach out into the world with your other senses. See if you can use the sense of hearing to notice the different sounds around you. Not just the ones in the room or in the house. Reach way up high and try to spot the sounds of an airplane that's flying above your head.

-Even more so, you can use your sense of taste or smell to try to notice anything that might put your entire body into alert. Not a desperate type of alert. Just a simple awakening, an opportunity to wake up entirely and focus on how the body is now.

-Without judging it, without thinking about it, just noticing how the body is. Great job! Now, we will be focusing on the central piece of the body and mind, and the most important piece of life about you and your being. The breath.

-I want you to take some DEEP, SERIOUS breaths in through the nose, and out through the mouth. Make them loud as if you'd want everybody in the room to know that you're taking some incredible, relaxing, awesome deep breaths.

-And as you do so, feel just how amazing it feels throughout the body to take these great big deep breaths! Feel how every muscle in the body gets a little less tensed. How any stress in the body and mind simply vanishes, like magic. Keep taking deep, controlled breaths for a few more moments now while getting even more comfortable in your spot.

-And with this last breath that you take, you'll gently close your eyes and let the breath come back to its natural pace, in and out through your nose. Gently observe as the breath calms down naturally, without you even having to do something about it. The human body knows a lot of amazing tricks, as you will learn during this game of meditation!

-Now that the breath has come back to the natural rhythm, it is time to play a game of visualization. Remember to always keep a gentle focus on the breath as we're moving along this practice. Regardless of what I'm asking you to do, always keep an eye on the breath, on how it feels to breath in and out and how it makes the entire body move.

-And while you do so, I want you to visualize that you're in your most ideal play and learning room in the world. Imagine a world filled with the toys you've always wanted. See them stacked one over the other all over the room, starting from the door all the way to the back of the room.

-Start by noticing the type of games that are in the room. Are there any puzzle games? Are there any car games, or drawing boards, or any balls or maybe a trampoline?

-Simply notice what sort of games are in the room and imagine yourself playing with the one you love most. It doesn't matter which game you chose as long as it is both awesome to play with and can also teach you something about life.

-I want you to visualize yourself playing with that game right now. And as you play, I want you to keep focusing on that sense of freedom, of acquiring new knowledge through playing. I want you to discover the powers of playing as a learning experience. Besides the fun aspect of play, there's a greater, learning-based experience you can get from it.

-Fully immerse yourself into the learning part of the game, whatever game you're playing right now. What does the game teach you? What are the lessons you can learn from it? Are they having something to do with life? Simply notice these things as you breath normally and keep a gentle focus of the expansion and contraction of your chest.

-As you're having fun with the game you're playing, look around and see if you can spot the books on the shelf right next to you in the room. Visualize the bookshelf in your mind. See the different colors of the book jackets, the titles and the authors' names.

-Take a moment to pause from your play and learn from it and mentally reach out to the books. Choose one book you think can improve your learning and playing abilities for your game. It doesn't matter the color, shape and size of the book, the name of the book or the author. Remember, you are the master of this mental exercise, you can have complete fun and freedom with it.

-Now that you've picked the book you want and gave it a name, open the book and see if there's something written inside its pages. You should see a great deal of text but some of the phrases are more important than others. There are especially ten phrases in the book that are very important for you to read.

-The first phrase reads "I can play and learn something at the same time no matter the game I'm enjoying". Read that one more time in the mind. "I can play AND learn something at the same time, no matter the game I'm enjoying".

-You are doing great, just keep breathing in and out through the nose. And if you're a little stuck or stiff, simply relax your shoulders, your legs, your head and neck and all of your body. Get a new sense of ease all through the body while you inhale and exhale through the nose.

-The second important phrase is right on the next page. It reads "I am curious; therefore, I am always learning something new by my nature". One more time, read it carefully in the mind. "I am curious; therefore, I am ALWAYS learning something new by my nature".

-Awesome, you are doing perfectly. These affirmations, as some call them, have immense power for you and will help you achieve more than you can think of in the future. Just remember to recall them whenever you're about to enjoy a new game from which you can learn things about life, yourself, and others.

-Let's go about and move to the third page in the book you chose, which we will be reading slowly and carefully, keeping our focus on what we're reading and nothing else. The phrase reads "I will become a better version of myself every time I learn something new". This one is very important so we will also read it a second time, also just in the mind. "I will become a BETTER version of myself, every time I learn something new.

-One of the reasons we add affirmations to these practices is, although they are simple phrases that might seem silly for some, when you're in a meditative state you've put your body and mind in such a way that it receives this information much quicker. You've enhanced your learning capabilities so much so that the phrase immediately sticks with you and is there for you whenever you're in doubt or distressed.

-We are now ready for the fourth affirmation of this practice. Let's listen to it carefully. It goes something like this: "Mistakes are not a bad thing. Each mistake can teach me a valuable lesson". Interesting, let's go about this one again, just to make sure it sticks. "Mistakes are not a bad thing. Each mistake can teach me a valuable lesson".

-The great thing about mistakes is, you never have to repeat them. But if you want to learn from them, see them for what they are. The trick with mistakes is to joyfully learn from them, not get too caught up in the mistake itself. Sure, the mistake might have not felt so good, but in life these things usually happen. It's fine, and life should go on every time.

-Very nicely done! You are really doing great so far with these affirmations. The fifth one comes up right now. Listen carefully! "I know I am on the right track when I can do hard things." Right, let's go over this one again, for a better understanding. "I know I am on the right track when I can do hard things."

-Being on the right track is not always an easy thing. For example, when you're going to school you have to keep on track, go to bed early to wake up rested, do your homework to be prepared for the next day, read and do some exercises to be ready. But going on with it, staying on track with things, will also have you able to do even the harder things that might pop up.

-We are now in the middle of the book you chose and the affirmations in it. I want you to put the book down for a few moments and concentrate on yourself again. Just briefly. Think of it as a mental pause in which we leave the mind to relax and to better assimilate the information that we've given it. The mind is like a sponge, as it pulls in everything that you feed it. This is why it's important to read or listen to only those pieces of information that will make your life better.

-Very well. Keep focusing on the breathing all the way through now, gently, just like if it were a game. We will resume the affirmations now.

-Wow, how time flies! We're on our sixth affirmation already! We'll be done with this session in no time for sure, and it's fun! Here's the next one, so listen carefully and become fully aware over the next few moments. "I cheer myself up when things get hard." One more for this short, yet important one. "I cheer myself up when things get hard."

-The purpose of life is to find your passion and thrive with it. Become the best musician, actor, writer, doctor, teacher, whatever you might be dreaming about doing later in your life. It all is possible, no matter how hard it might seem right now. The key is to remember to smile whenever things get hard. At school, at home, or in your group of friends. Cheering yourself up every time will keep your spirits up and lead you into making good decisions.

-For affirmation number 7, I've prepared one that I am sure you'll love. Ready? Here it comes: "I grow my brain by learning new things, even when I'm playing!" This affirmation literally means you should play more, regardless of what games you love. Here it goes one more time, just for the fun of it. "I grow my brain by learning new things, even when I'm playing!"

-Playing is a great tool for learning new things Puzzle games, mystery games, imagination games, sport games, geography quizzes or any trivia, they're all great for both fun and learning something new.

-Well, looks like we're at the eight affirmation now, which is great. It means we're closing in on this part of the meditation game. Exciting, right? Good, let's listen to this one and keep our focus there for now. "I can do anything that I set my mind to because I believe in myself without fail." This is a great one. A very important one. "I can do anything that I set my mind to because I believe in myself without fail."

-Setting your mind for something and then never going back is a great way to tackle your dreams. These dreams might look impossible now, but if you have the confidence it takes, you will find a way to follow through. Becoming something in life, becoming who you want to become in life, is nothing more than a combination of self-confidence and doing the things you need to do in order to turn into the person you want to be. It's that simple!

-Affirmation number nine is up next. Ready to listen to it? Alright, here it comes now. "I am smart and make good choices, which is why good things are happening in my life." One more time, for the books. "I am smart and make good choices, which is why good things are happening in my life."

-Good things sometimes just come to us. But for the most part, good things are a consequence of our choices and actions. There's an old saying that says "You make your own luck" and it's the best example to support this ninth affirmation today. Choices, smart choices, will simply create the premises for you to become lucky and to have good things happening all around you. It's an unwritten law that simply works and has always worked like this.

-Finally, we're at the last affirmation for the day. Are you ready for it? Become fully aware and focus on this one, as it is important and very rewarding. "I choose to have a great day today, tomorrow and every day forever!" Here it goes once more. "I choose to have a great day today, tomorrow and every day forever!"

-This is the best thing you can do with your life every day. Choose to have a great day today. Then, choose to have a great day tomorrow, and the day after, and so on. What happens around you is not in your control, and it will never be. But the way you choose to react to the stuff happening around you? That's 100% in your control. So why would you choose anything else but having a good day today?

-You may now close the book in your mind. You can put the book back on the shelf where it originally was and just relax while still in the room filled with great games. You can even enjoy another game or two and just play them in the mind while focusing on your breath at all times. Don't forget to do this, to recall the breath with each inhale, and then with each exhale.

-While still in the room that you've imagined for yourself right now, I want you to visualize a game that you've always wanted to play but never had the chance to. It could be a new board game that's just been released, or a sporting game, puzzle game, whatever it might be.

-As the game makes its appearance, I want you to visualize yourself playing the game. Fully emerging yourself into the action, into the story, into the mission. Enjoy this game to the fullest, enjoy every piece and every board section if it's a board game, enjoy every element if it's a sporting game, enjoy every piece of the puzzle if this is a puzzle game. Whatever it is, truly enjoy it.

-And as you do so, as you play along with your imagined game, what I want you to do is to simply relax to the best of your abilities. Relax. All there's to do now is to play the game, relax and nothing else. Think of it as your ultimate mission of this moment.

-Relax more and more as you play the game in your mind, your most prized gift. And as you relax, become more and more aware of the learning possibilities that the game is offering. Any game regardless of its form comes with a teachable purpose behind it. What is the lesson this game is providing for you?

-If you're playing a sporting game, maybe it has something to do with focus and strategy. Great, it's always a good thing to practice focusing your attention, or strategizing your next few moves. If you're playing a board game, again, you might be needed to focus on things like forms, colors, strategies and plans. Awesome! With puzzles, it's all about awareness and attention to details, to make sure every single piece fits where it's supposed to.

-Every single game, regardless of its nature, has a learning possibility behind it. In this state of complete relaxation and awareness, make it your goal to find those games that are the most teachable ones in existence. Play them every time you get the chance. Focus on the learning experiences of the games. Gather as much knowledge as you can. Focus on the ideas and the techniques that will help you not only excel in the game, but in life as well.

-It is now time to leave the room of games and learning. Remember to always keep this sense of learning through games and the liberty and knowledge it provides with you.

-We will also use a game to get back to our world and for this, all I want you to do is to pay a little attention to your body. It's very simple and it's a reversed process of the game that got us to remain calm and focused all throughout this meditation practice today. Here we go!

-I want you to start listening to your feet at first. How do your feet feel right now? If they're a little tense, that's fine as you've been sitting in the same place for a while now. If not, then it means you've chosen a great spot to sit in for our meditation game.

-Move up and see how are your knees doing right now? Are they achy, or relaxed? Simply observe the way the knees feel, the part of the body that helps you run, play with friends, jump on a trampoline or simply walk to school and back home.

-Awesome job, you are doing great! Remember to always keep a gentle focus on your breathing, which is naturally going in and out through the nose.

-We are now going to move up to the upper legs and the pelvic area, the center of the body. Simply notice how this part of your body feels right now. You don't have to do anything about it, just simply notice, and get ready to move on.

-Good. Now we will scan the stomach area, as well as the lower back. Observe these two parts of the body. How do they feel? Do they feel calm, peaceful? Is there any pain, or any stress in these parts of the body?

-Move up to the chest area now. Simply observe the way your chest feels, your lungs, and your heart. Is the heart beating normally? Is it a little slower, or maybe a little faster right now? The heart is the one pumping blood all over your body, bringing life throughout the entire thing. It is a very important organ and an amazing piece of biological machinery.

-You will now move to the head and start scanning it from the neck all the way up to the top of the hair. See if the neck has any stiffness through it. Then see if the face is making any grimace or not. Observe if the mind itself is calm or a little loud right now.

-Whatever it is that you discover, you don't have to do anything about it but just observe. You are here to learn about your body and mind. You are not here to command your body and mind. Just observe, take notice and move on to the next part. And so far, you've done great!

-We are now getting close to the end of this practice. Before we come back completely, I want you to get back slowly into the world using your senses of touch, smell and hearing.

-First, notice the weight of your body touching the chair that you're on, the floor or whatever it is that you're sitting on. Notice how the weight feels on these surfaces, how the points of contact between the body and the surfaces feel.

-Next, I want you to see if you can smell anything around in the room that you're in. See if you can spot a floral smell, or a food smell, whatever it is. Use your sense of smell to bring yourself back into the now, into the moment, out of the meditative state.

-Good! Now go ahead and use your sense of hearing and see if you can identify any sounds. They can be close sounds, like a TV running somewhere in the living room, or sounds coming from afar, like the rush of the outside street.

-And now, please take a deep breath in through the nose. And as you exhale through the mouth, slowly open your eyes and completely come back to the world around you.

-I hope you enjoyed this meditation game we've played here today. All through the rest of the day today and the following days, remember to find the learning experience from any activity that you'll be a part of. Regardless if it's a game, a class, a walk in the park or anything else. Simply seek and find the knowledge that you can grab from it and transform into something valuable for you as a person. And as you do so, whenever things become challenging, remember to find comfort in the simple act of observing your breath. Thank you for joining me and have an outstanding day!

Before we part, I would like to once again remind you that as a self-publishing author, reviews are the lifeblood of my work. I would be very happy and thankful if you could take a few moments to leave a review on Amazon. I truly appreciate your time.

REFERENCES

Brauer, J., Xiao, Y., Poulain, T., Friederici, AD., & Schirmer, A. *Frequency of Maternal Touch Predicts Resting Activity and Connectivity of the Developing Social Brain.* Cerebral Cortex, Volume 26, Issue 8, August 2016, Pages 3544–3552

Gabriel, G. (2001). *Will the real brain based learning please stand up.* Brain Connection.com Retrieved from https://brainconnection.brainhq.com/2001/08/26/will-the-real-brain-based-learning-please-stand-up/

Lillard, A., & Else-Quest, N. (2006, September 29). *Evaluating Montessori Education.* The journal Science.

Montessori, M. (1949). *The Absorbent Mind.* Adyar - Madras - India : Theosophical Publishing House

Montessori, M. (1909). *Discovery of the Child.* Dover Publications, Inc.

Montessori, M. (1909). The Montessori Method. New York Frederick A. Stokes Company

Montessori, M. (1936). *The Secret Childhood.* London. New York Longmans, Green and Co

National Association of Music Merchants (NAMM) Foundation. Retrieved from https://www.namm.org/

Stephenson, S. M. (2013). *The Joyful Child: Montessori, Global Wisdom for Birth to Three.* Michael Olaf Montessori Company.

The Parent Institute. (2014). Sitting still is important for kindergarten.

SchoolFamily.com. Retrieved from https://www.parent-institute.com/welcome.php

Werner, L. University Of Washington. (2001, May 30). *Babies Have A Different Way Of Hearing The World By Listening To All Frequencies Simultaneously*. ScienceDaily. Retrieved from www.sciencedaily.com/releases/2001/05/010529233110.htm

World Health Organization. Retrieved from https://www.who.int/topics/breastfeeding/en/

FURTHER RESOURCES

Agora Gaia. (2014, October 18). *Maria Montessori*
   https://www.youtube.com/watch?v=TXqeTYHn0p4

American Montessori Society. *Benefits of Montessori Education.*
   https://amshq.org/Families/Why-Choose-Montessori/Benefits-of-
   Montessori

American Montessori Society. (n.d). *Montessori Learning Materials.*
   https://amshq.org/About-Montessori/Inside-the-Montessori-
   Classroom/Infant-and-Toddler#montessori-learning-materials

Baker, I. (2017). *Music in the Montessori Classroom. Montessori* Services: A
   Resource for Preparing the Child's Environment.
   https://www.montessoriservices.com/ideas-insights/music-in-the-
   montessori-classroom

Brain Connection. (n.d). https://brainconnection.brainhq.com/

Chen, G. (2013). *10 Benefits of a Montessori Preschool.* Education.com
   https://www.education.com/magazine/article/10-benefits-
   montessori-preschool/

Chitwood, D. (2014, May 13). *The Montessori Weaning Table And Baby's
   First Solid Foods.* Living Montessori Now.
   https://livingmontessorinow.com/the-montessori-weaning-table-
   and-babys-first-solid-foods/

Daily Montessori: Bringing Montessori Education To Your Home.
   (n.d). *Language To Use When Talking To Infants.*

http://www.dailymontessori.com/language-development/language-used-when-talking-to-infants/

Daily Montessori: Bringing Montessori Education To Your Home. (n.d). *Language To Use When Talking To Toddlers.* http://www.dailymontessori.com/language-development/language-to-use-when-talking-to-toddlers/

Davidson, P. (2011, September 25). *The Magic of Grace & Courtesy.* MariaMontessori.com: A Project from Montessori Administrators Association. https://www.mariamontessori.com/2011/09/25/1645/

Davies, S. (n.d). *Age Appropriate Chores for Children.* The Montessori Notebook. https://www.themontessorinotebook.com/age-appropriate-chores-for-children/

Davies, S. (n.d). *How Not to Stop a Tantrum. Yes, You Read That Right.* The Montessori Notebook https://www.themontessorinotebook.com/stop-tantrum-yes-read-right/

Davies, S. (2015, May 29). *Montessori Art Trays for Toddlers.* Trillium Montessori Blog. https://www.trilliummontessori.org/montessori-art-trays-for-toddlers/

Davies, S. (n.d). *Montessori and Music.* The Montessori Notebook. https://www.themontessorinotebook.com/montessori-and-music/

Davies, S. (n.d). *Montessori Activities at 6 to 9 months.* The Montessori Notebook. https://www.themontessorinotebook.com/montessori-activities-6-9-months/

Davies, S. (n.d). *The ultimate list of Montessori activities for babies, toddlers and preschoolers.* The Montessori Notebook. https://www.themontessorinotebook.com/montessori-activities-for-babies-toddlers-and-preschoolers/

Davies, S. (n.d). *What? Montessori for babies?* The Montessori Notebook https://www.themontessorinotebook.com/montessori-for-babies/

Eden Prairie Montessori. (2018, April 6). *15 Awesome Montessori Instagram Accounts You Need to Follow.* https://edenprairiemontessori.com/15-awesome-montessori-instagram-accounts-you-need-to-follow/

Ellis, M., & the KHM Staff. (2014, December 7). *Positive Communication with Children.* https://www.kinderhousemontessori.com/positive-communication-with-children-2/

Emily. (n.d). *Education Through Movement.* The Age of Montessori. http://ageofmontessori.org/education-through-movement/

Emily. (n.d). *6 Great Ways to Create a Learning Environment at Home.* The Age of Montessori. http://ageofmontessori.org/6-great-ways-to-create-a-learning-environment-at-home/

Epstein, P. (2016, January 15). *The Sensitive Periods.* Rochester Montessori School

How children learn influences who they will become. https://rmschool.org/content/sensitive-periods

FeedSpot. (2019, December 11). *Top 100 Montessori Blogs And Websites To Follow in 2019.* https://blog.feedspot.com/montessori_blogs/

How We Montessori. (2016). Eight Awesome Montessori Families to Follow on Instagram. https://www.howwemontessori.com/how-we-montessori/2016/05/montessori-families-to-follow-on-instagram.html

Irinyi, M. (2009, March 18). *The Six Principles of the Montessori Prepared Environment Explained.* NAMC Montessori Teaching Training Blog. https://montessoritraining.blogspot.com/2009/03/principles-of-montessori-prepared.html

Jacobs, J.M. (2014). *Movement Enhances Learning.* Montessori Services: A Resource for Preparing the Child's Environment. https://www.montessoriservices.com/at-home

Kavanaugh, N. (2016). *Benefits of the Montessori Weaning Table.* The Kavanaugh Report.

http://www.thekavanaughreport.com/2016/02/benefits-of-montessori-weaning-table.html?m=1

MariaMontessori.com: A Project from Montessori Administrators Association. (n.d). *Infant/Toddler.* https://www.mariamontessori.com/learn/infant/

Maria Montessori International Academy. (2017, December 18). *Teaching Your Baby with the Montessori Method.* https://inmontessori.com/montessori-method-15-tips-make-baby-smarter/

Maunz, M.E. (n.d). *Motor Education & Exercises of Practical Life.* The Age of Montessori. http://ageofmontessori.org/motor-education-exercises-of-practical-life/

Maunz, M.E. (n.d). *Sensitive Periods in Development.* The Age of Montessori. http://ageofmontessori.org/sensitive-periods-in-development/

Maunz, M.E. (n.d). *The Absorbent Mind.* The Age of Montessori. http://ageofmontessori.org/the-absorbent-mind/

Montessori Academy at Sharon Springs. (2019, February 4). *Physical Development in a Montessori Preschool.* https://montessoriacademysharonsprings.com/physical-development-in-a-montessori-preschool/

Montessori Australia. (2019, October 29). *Outdoor Environment.* https://montessori.org.au/blog/outdoor-environment

Montessori Australia. (2017, March 20). *Parenting Tips: From Feeding to Eating.* https://montessori.org.au/blog/parenting-tips-feeding-eating

Montessori Compass. (n.d). *Montessori Scope and Sequence: Art, Music, and Movement.* https://montessoricompass.com/art-music-movement/

Montessori Guide: Delving Deeper Into Our Practice. (n.d). *Capturing Ordinary Days: The Child's Work.* https://montessoriguide.org/the-childs-work

Montessori, M,. (n.d). *Six "Sensitive Periods".* https://www.montessoritrainingusa.com/sites/montessoritrainingu sa.com/files/Six%20Sensitive%20Periods.pdf (Retrieved from Montessori Teacher Education Center San Francisco Bay Area. https://www.montessoritrainingusa.com/)

Montessori Services: A Resource for Preparing the Child's Environment. (2019). *At Home.* https://www.montessoriservices.com/at-home

NAMC Montessori Teaching Training Blog. (2013, November 12). *A Free Flowing Montessori Environment — Indoors and Outdoors.* https://montessoritraining.blogspot.com/2013/11/a-free-flowing-montessori-environment.html

NAMC Montessori Teaching Training Blog. (2013, July 19). *Modern Materials Used in the Infant/Toddler Environment.* https://montessoritraining.blogspot.com/2013/07/modern-montessori-materials-infant-toddler-prepared-environment.html

NAMC Montessori Teaching Training Blog. (2010, March 03). *Montessori Grace and Courtesy: Lesson Resources for Infants, Toddlers & Preschoolers.* https://montessoritraining.blogspot.com/2010/03/montessori-grace-courtesy-infants.html

NAMC Montessori Teaching Training Blog. (2010, March 31). *Motor Skills and Movement in the Infant / Toddler Montessori Prepared Environment* https://montessoritraining.blogspot.com/2010/03/movement-in-montessori-infanttoddler.html

NAMC Montessori Teaching Training Blog. (2014, April 25). *The Absorbent Mind, Chapter 13: The Importance of Movement.* https://montessoritraining.blogspot.com/2014/04/absorbent-mind-ch13-importance-of-movement-studying-montessori.html

Nienhuis Montessori. (n.d). *Infant/Toddler 0-3.*

https://www.nienhuis.com/int/en/furniture-for-infant-toddler-0-3/page/2829/

Nienhuis Montessori. (n.d). *Infant/Toddler 0-3/Movement*
https://www.nienhuis.com/int/en/movement-for-infant-toddler-0-3/page/2822/#/?CPI=2

Nienhuis Montessori. (n.d). *Infant/Toddler 0-3/Practical Life*.
https://www.nienhuis.com/int/en/practical-life-for-infant-toddler-0-3/page/2821/#/?CPI=2

North American Montessori Center (NAMC). (n.d). *Communicating with Children the Montessori Way*.
https://www.montessoritraining.net/docs/default-source/infant-toddler-curriculum/namc-it-guide-sample.pdf

Philipart, H,. *An Introduction to Practical Life*. Montessori Guide: Delving Deeper Into Our Practice. https://montessoriguide.org/an-introduction-to-practical-life

Printed in Great Britain
by Amazon